Editor-in-Chief and Founder:
   Lyndon H. LaRouche, Jr.
Editorial Board: *Lyndon H. LaRouche, Jr. , Helga
   Zepp-LaRouche, Robert Ingraham, Tony
   Papert, Gerald Rose, Dennis Small, Jeffrey
   Steinberg, William Wertz*
Co-Editors: *Robert Ingraham, Tony Papert*
Technology: *Marsha Freeman*
Transcriptions: *Katherine Notley*
Ebooks: *Richard Burden*
Graphics: *Alan Yue*
Photos: *Stuart Lewis*
Circulation Manager: *Stanley Ezrol*

INTELLIGENCE DIRECTORS
Economics: *Marcia Merry Baker, Paul Gallagher*
History: *Anton Chaitkin*
Ibero-America: *Dennis Small*
Russia and Eastern Europe: *Rachel Douglas*
United States: *Debra Freeman*

INTERNATIONAL BUREAUS
Bogotá: *Miriam Redondo*
Berlin: *Rainer Apel*
Copenhagen: *Tom Gillesberg*
Lima: *Sara Madueño*
Melbourne: *Robert Barwick*
Mexico City: *Gerardo Castilleja Chávez*
New Delhi: *Ramtanu Maitra*
Paris: *Christine Bierre*
Stockholm: *Ulf Sandmark*
United Nations, N.Y.C.: *Leni Rubinstein*
Washington, D.C.: *William Jones*
Wiesbaden: *Göran Haglund*

ON THE WEB
e-mail: eirns@larouchepub.com
www.larouchepub.com
www.executiveintelligencereview.com
www.larouchepub.com/eiw
Webmaster: *John Sigerson*
Assistant Webmaster: *George Hollis*
Editor, Arabic-language edition: *Hussein Askary*

EIR (ISSN 0273-6314) *is published weekly
(50 issues), by EIR News Service, Inc.,
P.O. Box 17390, Washington, D.C. 20041-0390.
(703) 297-8434*

European Headquarters: E.I.R. GmbH, Postfach
Bahnstrasse 9a, D-65205, Wiesbaden, Germany
Tel: 49-611-73650
Homepage: http://www.eir.de
e-mail: info@eir.de
Director: Georg Neudecker

Montreal, Canada: 514-461-1557
eir@eircanada.ca

Denmark: EIR - Danmark, Sankt Knuds Vej 11,
basement left, DK-1903 Frederiksberg, Denmark.
Tel.: +45 35 43 60 40, Fax: +45 35 43 87 57. e-mail:
eirdk@hotmail.com.

Mexico City: EIR, Sor Juana Inés de la Cruz 242-2
Col. Agricultura C.P. 11360
Delegación M. Hidalgo, México D.F.
Tel. (5525) 5318-2301
eirmexico@gmail.com

Postmaster: Send all address changes to *EIR*, P.O.
Box 17390, Washington, D.C. 20041-0390.

Signed articles in *EIR* represent the views of the authors,
and not necessarily those of the Editorial Board.

The 2018 Branching Point in History

ECB Stages Coup Against Legitimate Government of Italy, Markets in Despair

by Liliana Gorini, Chairwoman of MoviSol, the LaRouche Movement of Italy

May 29—In an intervention which violated the most fundamental rules of democracy and international law, on May 27 the hierarchy of the European Union (EU) vetoed the "government of change" which was being formed in Italy, and which had just won a clear parliamentary majority from the voters. Instead, the EU has imposed yet another technocratic government, which had been ready for months, led by "Mr. Spending Review," Carlo Cottarelli, whose only plan is to cut the debt, and who has the support only of the Democratic Party, which lost the legislative elections of March 4.

This is the most recent example of that "suspension of democracy," demanded years ago by the EU, when it introduced the balanced budget as the only aim of each and every European government, as in the "market-conformed democracy" of Germany's Angela Merkel.

The most paradoxical aspects, which have no precedent in the history of the Italian Republic—a parliamentary Republic and not a Presidential one—are the reasons given by the President of the Republic, Sergio Mattarella, to explain why he vetoed Professor Paolo Savona, a renowned economist, former minister, and former head of the employers' federation, Confindustria, as Finance Minister of the new government. Mattarella said he did this in order not to upset "foreign investors" who fear that Italy might leave the Euro. This, despite the fact that in the government program agreed to between the two victorious parties, the Lega and the Five-Star Party, and also in the statement of Professor Savona of last Sunday, there was no mention

of leaving the Euro. Rather, they demanded a change from the failed policy of austerity, which provoked "poverty, reduced incomes and inequality" in Italy, in Professor Savona's words.

In the days before this unacceptable coup against a legitimate government, a government which had been awaited with great hope by the Italians, Mattarella was apparently often in touch with the head of the European Central Bank (ECB) Mario Draghi, that Mario Draghi who in 2011 had imposed on Italy the technocratic government of Mario Monti, not elected by any Italian, along with a letter which dictated the tasks of that government. French President Macron also interfered, by calling up the new Premier, Giuseppe Conte, before he was received at the Quirinale Presidential Palace with his list of ministers, to ask him to remove Paolo Savona from that list. The next day Macron supported Mattarella in rejecting Savona.

The "fake news" press which speaks for the City of London and the financial lobbies, whose speculation was responsible for the 2008 crisis, permitted itself to insult not only the Lega and the Five Star Party, who had worked together to forge a government program aimed at promoting jobs and fighting poverty, but all Italians as a people, calling them "barbarians" (*Financial Times*) and "freeloaders" (*Der Spiegel*). "Europe" did not like the immediate reaction to these insults, of the Lega's Matteo Salvini ("Better barbarians than slaves!"), or the Five Star Party's Luigi Di Maio ("How dare they?"). The day after Mattarella's coup, which was in no way justified by the Italian Constitution, the

German financial daily *Handelsblatt* ran the headline, "The President of the Republic Did It Right, Forza Mattarella!"

The question many are asking is: Why impose by force a technocratic government which will last not more than three months, since it does not have a majority in Parliament, and which, according to Democratic Party politician Massimo D'Alema, will increase the votes of the Lega-Five Star government coalition from 60% to 80%? Are financial markets so desperate to buy time, even if only three months?

This seems to be the real reason for the *coup d'etat*. Deutsche Bank is on the verge of bankruptcy; its exposure to derivatives has reached such a level that even its chief economist, David Folkerts-Landau, has had to admit that it has become a hedge fund. As Italian economist Alberto Bagnai, elected to the Italian Senate with the Lega, declared in a radio interview, "The Euro could blow up, but not because of us. Deutsche Bank is ready to fire 7,000 employees, and all of these big banks have heavy derivatives exposure. Let's suppose that German private finance will blow up instead of the Italian public debt. We have to be ready for such an event."

Five-Star Party leader Alessandro Di Battista, interviewed May 28 on prime-time national television by Lilli Gruber, said "They blocked this government because they are terrified of banking separation and a state investment bank."

Thus, rather than the fear of an Italexit, what freaked out the markets was the fact that the Salvini-Di Maio government had two points in its program which are dear to the LaRouche movement—reinstating Glass-Steagall, and national banking in order to issue credit for the real economy. The present financial system is so rotten and so ready to explode, that it does not allow discussion of such issues, let alone their inclusion in the government program of an important country such as Italy, one of the founders of Europe. In order to keep this rotten system alive, previous Italian governments, from Monti to Gentiloni, have imposed draconian austerity measures.

"Europe," the EU, the Troika, the ECB, and the economic and press outlets of the establishment refuse to understand that in recent years a New Paradigm has been asserting itself, and has found its expression in the Brexit, in Trump's election victory in the United States, in the "No" vote in the Italian constitutional referendum, and now in the Italian elections of March 4. It also finds its expression in the fact that two thirds of the world has joined the Belt and Road Initiative of China's President Xi Jinping, with its win-win policy of economic cooperation, as opposed to the geopolitical policy of confrontation with Russia and China leading to war.

For the moment, they have managed to stop the government of change, which will be back again in a few months anyway, as Salvini said, but they cannot stop the New Paradigm, which is asserting itself all over the world. As to the "foreign investors" and their worries about our country, let me I repeat here what I have been repeating for years in interviews and articles: Markets should not be reassured–rather, they should be jailed, for provoking the suicide of two pensioners who lost all their savings in the banking crisis. For imposing the bail-in, which means the theft of our savings.

President Mattarella declared that he vetoed this government in order to protect our savings. The only way to protect our savings is not by obeying the *diktat* of Brussels, but rather by adopting LaRouche's Four Laws, which may be very briefly summarized for our purposes here, as: 1. Glass-Steagall; 2. National Banking; 3. A Credit system; and 4. A Fusion economy. We therefore call on the "new government of change" to adopt these Four Laws, for the moment only in the Italian Parliament, while waiting for early elections in autumn, whereafter it will finally be sworn in. This will also be a reply in kind to the speculative financial interests which torpedoed this government.

EIRContents

www.larouchepub.com   Volume 45, Number 22, June 1, 2018

*Cover
This Week*

*Sergio Mattarella,
President of Italy
(center), May 27,
2018.*

Palazzo del Quirinale

THE 2018 BRANCHING POINT IN HISTORY

ZEPP-LAROUCHE WEBCAST

The Worm Has Turned: Will Obama Administration Join Leading Brits on Trial as the Real 'Collusion' Is Exposed?

This is the edited transcript of the May 24, 2018 Schiller Institute New Paradigm webcast, an interview with the founder of the Schiller Institutes, Helga Zepp-LaRouche. She was interviewed by Harley Schlanger. A video *of the webcast is available.*

Harley Schlanger: Hello. I'm Harley Schlanger from the Schiller Institute. Welcome to this week's international webcast featuring our founder and President, Helga Zepp-LaRouche.

We are in the midst of a series of unfolding developments, and we'll address them in the context of the discussion today. There are a number of things happening, each of which is very significant, and we don't have full readings yet. But we want to start with what I think is something most people are not aware of—the coming earthquake that is hitting Europe, in this case from the Italian election. The new government is being put together, and there's a strong, negative reaction from the European Union, for good reason. Helga, what is the significance of these Italian developments, in the context of the overall strategic situation?

Helga Zepp-LaRouche: We have now a new prime minister, Giuseppe Conte, who is a politically unknown law professor. But the gentleman the EU ministers find most disturbing is the mooted new Finance Minister, the 81-year-old Paolo Savona, a well-established economist. In the beginning, Savona was completely for the euro, but when he saw the consequences for Italy of the single currency, he became completely anti-euro, and he has demanded a "Plan B" for Italy, meaning leaving the euro. He has also called the euro a "German prison" for Italy, and has given it some even worse names.

So the negative reaction is quite incredible. All kinds of people, politicians, and media have threatened Italy with financial warfare. One guy said the markets will teach Italy a lesson and bring it back to the path of virtue. One of the key anchors of the 2nd TV channel in Germany, Claus Kleber, a real specimen of his profession, to put it very diplomatically, said one should use

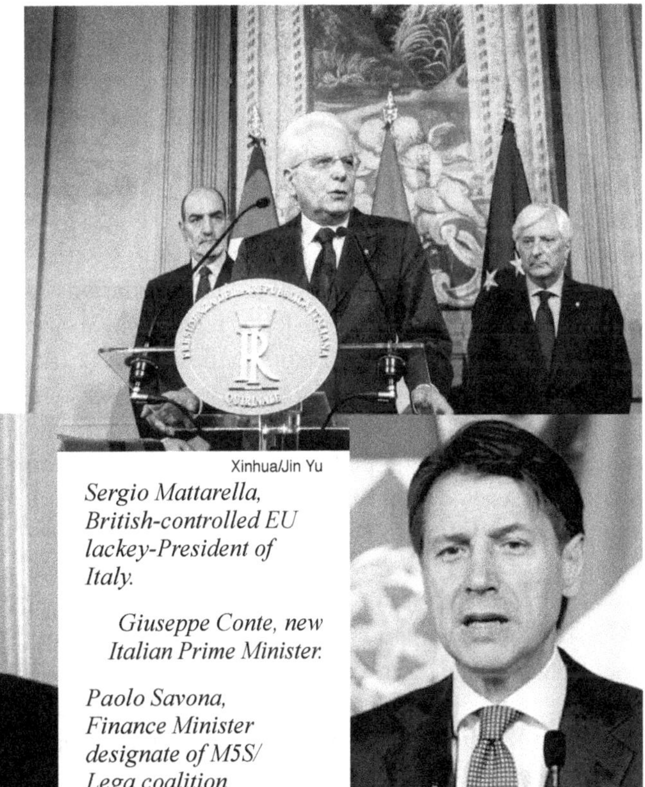

Xinhua/Jin Yu

Sergio Mattarella, British-controlled EU lackey-President of Italy.

Giuseppe Conte, new Italian Prime Minister.

Paolo Savona, Finance Minister designate of M5S/ Lega coalition government.

Creative Commons

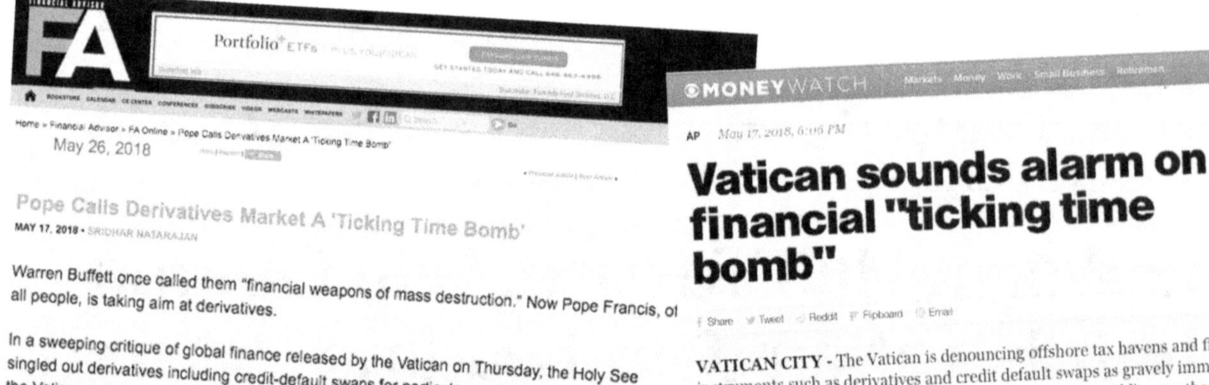

the gag bit—a torturous bit for horses which no good horseman would ever use, because it really tortures the horse—to discipline Italy.

This is incredible. Here are people who are constantly making the hugest complaints about China lacking democracy and what not, but in this case they're openly calling for regime change and advocating the use of warfare techniques against one of their own European Union members.

Now, I think if Savona indeed becomes finance minister, people are in for some surprises, because he is a very experienced person; he's not a lightweight, as the media are saying about Prime Minister Giuseppe Conte. This is not an isolated phenomenon. It's not Italy that is causing the financial crisis. Italy's election result is only the latest in a long arc of revolt against the neo-liberal policies expressed in the Brexit, in the election of Donald Trump, in the "no" to the Italian referendum changing the Constitution last year, in the Austrian election, and now in the Italian election. All these cases express in some fashion the will of the populations to no longer submit to unjust austerity regimes that only benefit the banks, the speculators, and the rich, at the expense of the masses of the population.

Therefore this is a very important moment, and rather than being completely shocked about it, and having hysterical tantrums. I think the opportunity should be exploited to take advantage of the positive elements of the new government in Italy, where both coalition partners, the Lega and the 5 Star Movement (M5S) have in their party platforms, and now also in the coalition contract, two of Lyndon LaRouche's basic laws: namely, the implementation of Glass-Steagall, and secondly, the creation of National Banking to channel investments into the real economy. So, rather than being hysterical about this, one should take it as a

golden opportunity to get rid of the extremely dangerous speculative excesses and go for a unified Glass-Steagall separation of the banks as a first step and start to save the system in this way.

In one sense, this crisis in Italy can provide an opportunity to make an urgent change in this direction.

Schlanger: Helga, I would just like to make a point of something you brought up, which is that the people who are arguing against these policies are essentially saying that the voters have no right to express an opinion if it goes against the policies of the bankers. The line from the media is that we're in the midst of a robust recovery, things are improving, the European economy is improving. But the voters are voting to show that they don't believe that. And there are other important developments, for example the continuing problems with the Macron government in France, and Deutsche Bank's continuing to be at the top of this list of the world's most endangered banks. I'd like you to just emphasize that the crisis of the real economy is what's behind the revolt, and that's why the Four Laws concept of Lyndon LaRouche is so crucial.

Zepp-LaRouche: A May 17 editorial carried by the website https://www.MauldinEconomics.com warns of the consequences of the corporate debt bubble, which is much, much worse than in 2008. They're warning of a new financial crisis of "biblical dimensions." Now, I don't know—"biblical dimensions," that's the Deluge, or some other fundamental crisis like that. And then you have the ongoing crisis around Argentina; Turkey's lira is falling, forcing the central banks to reverse their interest rate policies. So this is all extremely fragile.

What just happened at Deutsche Bank (DB) is very indicative that there is an understanding that some changes must be made. Two years ago, when Deutsche Bank was already in a severe crisis, my husband, Lyndon LaRouche, demanded that Deutsche Bank change its entire policy since 1989, since the assassination of its director, Alfred Herrhausen, and go back to Herrhausen's model of industrial banking. At that point, many people thought that this would never happen, that Deutsche Bank was a hopeless case. But while I don't want to make a final judgment on it, it is a fact that last month, the leadership of Deutsche Bank kicked out its CEO, John Cryan. And then, in *Handelsblatt*, the chief economist of Deutsche Bank, David Folkerts-Landau, gave a long interview describing how it was a big mistake, over the past two decades, to have shifted the entire investment profile of Deutsche Bank into only investment banking, going into derivatives trading. He makes some correct points, namely that Merrill Lynch was brought in, and a team which basically allowed a reverse takeover of Deutsche Bank, so that it became completely foreign controlled and directed, oriented to high-risk speculation—I think it still has a portfolio of something like $46 trillion in derivatives outstanding, making DB the largest derivatives bank in the world.

At a Deutsche Bank shareholder meeting today they also apparently tried to kick out Paul Achleitner, the supervisory board chairman of Deutsche Bank. The only thing I can say about Folkerts-Landau is that, as several insiders told us, he was one of the people who was involved in changing the bank's profile to make it solely an investment bank. He did not criticize that change for the last two decades, and *Spiegel Online* even says that Achleitner's recent criticism of the policy he formerly held was to put on a *mea culpa* show of self-criticism so that he would not be kicked out.

I think that's true. The new chief executive is Christian Sewing, who has been at the bank since 1989. It's being rumored that Sewing will totally concentrate on making investments in the real economy inside Germany a priority, thus turning Deutsche Bank back into a commercial bank at the service of industry. We have to see if that actually happens, but I think the shares were already below 10 euros, the red line when Deutsche Bank is in danger of going bankrupt.

Anyway, I'm just saying that we are on the verge of a new financial crisis. We are sitting on a volcano. A couple of weeks ago, the Vatican's Congregation for the

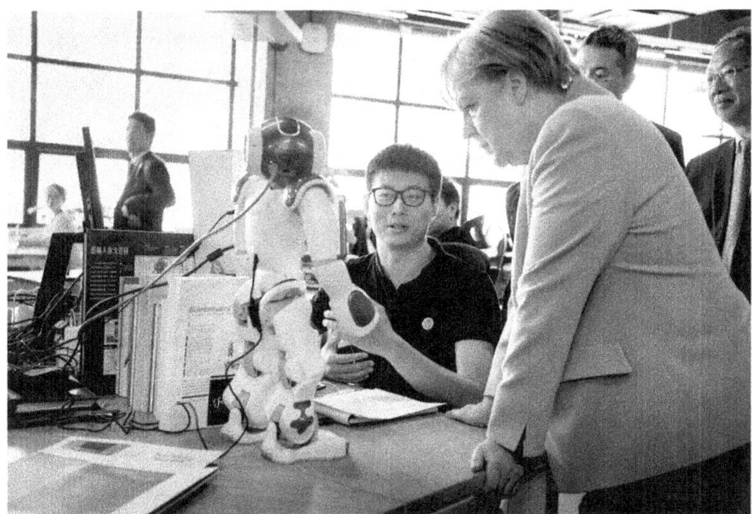

German Chancellor Angela Merkel in China, May 26, 2018.

Doctrine of the Faith put out a paper saying that derivatives are a ticking time-bomb and condemning derivatives trading as morally and economically completely unacceptable, because it just makes the rich richer and makes losses for everybody else. Warnings are also coming from Thomas Hoenig, President of the Federal Reserve Bank, Kansas City (1991-2011) and Vice Chairman of the FDIC (2012-2018); Sheila Bair, Chairman of the FDIC (2006-2011); and many others.

The Italian developments, as I said, have provided a new opportunity to get rid of the excesses of the derivatives trading; go instead for banking separation, and the more such action is taken in a coordinated fashion, the better, and it must occur really quickly.

Schlanger: Speaking of Germany, the Chancellor of Germany is in China. Any chance that the weakened and beleaguered Angela Merkel will come back with a New Silk Road Spirit?

Zepp-LaRouche: Well—[laughs] I don't think so. The Chinese, as they did with the Trump Administration, will promise more opening up for finance, for cooperation concerning e-cars and similar things, such as automatic driving cars; so I think they will come back with some kind of a package. Merkel made the statement, quoted everywhere, that she regards the rise of China as the biggest challenge for the remaining years of her being in office as Chancellor. As long as she retains that attitude, she won't get much.

She is typical of the people who on the one hand see that without China nothing functions any more in the world. But on the other, she is a really hard-core geopolitician in her attitude towards Russia, and she also always regards China as a rival, so it's a mixed situation. I would be very happy if she comes back brimming with the New Silk Road Spirit, but I have my doubts.

Schlanger: Now we come to probably the most complex of the situations, which is that in the United States. President Trump has just announced this afternoon, that he is cancelling the summit with Kim Jong-un. But this is occurring at a very interesting time, in which the British role in Russiagate, in the attacks on Trump, is in the open. Why don't we start with that? Because this is something that we have been fighting for, going back to the dossier that we put out on Robert Mueller. Based on the investigations that we launched, we insisted that Christopher Steele must not be seen as an isolated case, but as part of a British-directed assault against the United States:

White House/Pete Souza

President Obama and his CIA Director John Brennan.

This situation is moving fairly quickly, isn't it, Helga?

Zepp-LaRouche: Yes. As a matter of fact, President Trump's recent tweets are quite to the point, namely that "Russiagate" has turned into "Spygate"; that there has been absolutely no proof of any collusion on the part of the Trump campaign or Trump Presidency with Russia, but it is instead the very people involved in the coup attempt who have woven a spiderweb of collusion among the heads of the intelligence agencies of the Obama Administration with British intelligence, and that there has been an ongoing effort by British intelligence figures, even before any investigation officially started, to connect with all kinds of persons in the Trump election team, to try to somehow involve them in some kind of a connection with some Russians. All of this is coming out now.

So, long before the Trump election victory, or even the nomination, there was a clear effort by British intel-

DIA/Staff Sgt. Jonathan Lovelady

Anti-Trump cabal of Obama Intelligence chiefs testifying before House Permanent Select Committee on Intelligence: (l. to r.) James Comey, FBI Director; John Brennan, CIA Director; James Clapper, Director of National Intelligence.

ligence to lay leads, to create paper trails, to manufacture and orchestrate the situation, in order to hang a made-up "collusion with Russia" on the Trump campaign, and Trump himself. And this is all now coming out.

This is now subject to public discussions. For example, on Monday, Trump met with several Justice Department and intelligence officials—Deputy Attorney General Rod Rosenstein, FBI Director Christopher Wray, and Director of National Intelligence Dan Coates, in the White House, to review "highly classified and other information he had requested" related to the Russia investigation. And today, as a follow-up, Trump's Chief of Staff John Kelly is meeting with the CIA, the FBI, the Department of Justice, together with congressmen—for example, Rep. Devin Nunes, Sen. Chuck Grassley—and they're now getting access to all the documents, including Rosenstein's memorandum defining the scope of Special Counsel Robert Mueller's investigation. All these documents will now be made available to the respective investigative committees in the House and Senate. The activities revealed in these documents constitute criminal violations of law and the Constitution, so this is big!

I think Trump may absolutely be right when he tweeted yesterday, "SPYGATE could be one of the biggest political scandals in history!" It is now clear that there was a task force involving an institutional group of people who orchestrated all of this, in a presidential election campaign. Trump said that what was done against Bernie Sanders also was done on a much larger scale against him.

When all of this comes out, I think the world will really be a different place, and I think when President Trump is freed of this spiderweb, he will be in a much better position to carry through with his intentions than you have seen so far.

Schlanger: What you're describing is technically called "entrapment," that the FBI—or, actually, John Brennan, James Clapper, and then James Comey later, were all involved in colluding with the British intelligence services, the GCHQ, MI5, and MI6 to create Russiagate. The key people in that operation are being named now, such as Stefan Halper, Joseph Mifsud, and Alexander Downer, the current Australian High Commissioner to Great Britain—all tied to MI5, MI6, and

various private agencies. This was brought up by Sen. Rand Paul at the hearings, when he asked CIA head nominee Gina Haspel whether or not the CIA was involved in getting evidence from Britain. So a lot of this is coming out.

To what extent, Helga, is this then connected to the financial crisis? Make the connection for people, because there's still some confusion about how the financial crisis is then intersecting this operation against Trump because of Trump's willingness to work with Russia and China.

Zepp-LaRouche: The big concern, pro and con, is China's rising, its strategic partnership with Russia, and that the New Silk Road now involves 140 nations. And, as many statistics have shown, the New Silk Road dynamic is already creating a completely new paradigm: economic growth and a dynamic in science, technology and innovation. So the real momentum in many, many fields is with the alignments among Russia, China, now India, Japan, the Shanghai Cooperation Organization, the BRICS, the China-Latin America CELAC connection, and the Chinese investments in Africa. So, this has created a completely different dynamic in the world.

Now look at the condition of Wall Street, the condition in the City of London, and the absolute turmoil in the European Union. Seeing the rise of China, the geopoliticians are absolutely desperate to keep their model. But they're incapable of recognizing the causes for the loss of their grip on the world and are therefore unable to correct their policies.

As I said earlier, the Italy attackers right now, completely fail to even ask, why is it that the two euro-critic parties had the best electoral results? It is the same reason—and I want to repeat this—it is the same reason Britons voted to have the UK leave the European Union, the same reason the people in the Midwest voted for Trump and against Hillary Clinton, and the same reason there is an absolutely hysterical effort by people who have made gigantic, virtual fortunes—sometimes it's not so virtual, but sometimes it's, indeed, just virtual fortunes—with this highly speculative system, the neo-liberal system connected with wars based on lies, with so-called "humanitarian interventions," regime changes, and color revolutions. That whole model is really not functioning any more.

President Trump won the election because he promised that he would no longer have the United States engage in senseless foreign wars. The neo-cons in his administration have never let up in their efforts to lure him back. And therefore, I think Trump's cancelling, or postponing, the summit with Kim Jong-un is really unfortunate, because it would have been far better to make one clear step for peace. Obviously, there were difficulties, in terms of the procedures for the denuclearization, for example, 2015. Today the international press was invited to see the destruction of North Korea's nuclear test site. So North Korea has made a number of goodwill gestures. Therefore, I think it's very regrettable that this meeting was postponed. But hopefully it will come back on the agenda.

But the real connection is the fight between the dysfunctional old paradigm, and the New Paradigm, which is focussed on the common good of the people and on general economic growth. And just as an additional element: China has just completely but Kim Jong-un had released three Americans, one of whom had been detained since

abandoned its two-child per family policy, saying that there has been a change in the view about population—that in the past, when they adopted the one-child, and then two-child policies, the thinking then was that additional children are a *burden* in an economy with limited resources. But now they have changed their view and see each new child, especially every young person, as a tremendous *asset* of creative power, of additional richness of the entire society.

Looking at the difference in these two world views, you can readily see that this is a fundamental fight going

Xinhua/Cheng Dayu

North Korean nuclear test site of Punggye-ri, destroyed by the North Korean government on May 24, 2018, as one of the confidence-building measures preliminary to the Trump/Kim Jung-un summit.

on for mankind's ability to govern itself in a reasonable way. However, the danger of a financial collapse still hangs over the world, at least concerning very much the trans-Atlantic part. So I think LaRouche's Four Laws policy is the absolutely urgent policy of the hour.

Schlanger: In terms of these two paradigms, look at what just happened near my old home town of Houston, Texas, where another one of these mass shootings has just occurred in Santa Fe High School. School shootings have almost become commonplace in the United States; whereas in China, there is a total emphasis on education, on science.

This goes back to one of the fundamental economic breakthroughs of your husband: the concept of potential relative population-density, a concept opposed by people such as Prince Philip, the genocidal Consort of Queen Elizabeth (if he's still breathing), his whole life.

Helga, in this sense, I assume you see this change in China as an absolutely significant recognition of, again, the difference between the two paradigms, but also your husband's view of this concept of potential relative population-density.

Zepp-LaRouche: Yes. The Chinese have clearly totally changed, starting with Deng Xiaoping and his reforms after the Cultural Revolution. Especially in the last five, six years with the leadership of Xi Jinping, there has been an absolute understanding about the fun-

President Trump Should Hold Early Summit with Russian President Putin

By Edward Lozansky and Jim Jatras - Monday, May 21, 2018

ANALYSIS/OPINION:

WE THE PEOPLE ASK THE FEDERAL GOVERNMENT TO PROPOSE A NEW ADMINISTRATION POLICY:

President Donald Trump should hold early summit with Russian President Vladimir Putin

Created by J.J. on May 21, 2018

Ronald Reagan famously said: "A nuclear war cannot be won and must never be fought. The only value in our two nations possessing nuclear weapons is to make sure they will never be used." Unfortunately, today a new Cold War between the US and Russia again poses an existential threat to the people of both nations and to the whole world. Therefore, we urge President Trump to follow in the steps of Donald Reagan and to start a direct dialogue with

Sign This Petition

Needs **99,533 signatures** by June 20, 2018 to get a response from the White House

damental issues of life—he has given the task to the Chinese scientists to find out how the human mind works, determining the origin and importance of life in the universe; and discovering the laws of the universe. He has especially encouraged an emphasis on innovation, on creativity, in education as the sources of wealth. And now as they see the connection between qualitative advances in knowledge of physical laws and the ability to have more people, and more people again, leading to more creativity, I think they are absolutely on the right track.

Schlanger: Well, we didn't have a whole lot of time to talk before the program, so if there's something else that you wanted to bring up, you have a chance. Is there anything else on your radar screen?

Zepp-LaRouche: Yes: there is a petition on the website of the White House, initiated by Professor Edward Lozansky, founder and president of the American University in Moscow, and Jim Jatras, a former U.S. diplomat and foreign policy adviser to the Senate Republican leadership, calling for an early summit between President Trump and President Putin. They make essentially the same point that we have been making for the last several months. President Trump is still so much up against neocons in the Republican Party. He's really

done a remarkable job under the circumstances, with the entire intelligence apparatus against him, not only what is called the "deep state," which is really an incorrect characterization, because of the role of British intelligence acting on behalf of the British monarchy against the United States.

In order to cut through all this—given the fact that the entire Russiagate operation was intended to prevent a good relationship between Russia and the United States, which Trump all the time said would be a "good thing and not a bad thing," and he tries to do it—the Trump/Putin summit should go forward soon, which the petition urges.

So, I call on all of you who are listening, or watching, to sign this petition urging that such an early summit take place. I think this petition is an absolutely important initiative, and if it gathers more than 100,000 signatures by June 20 (within 30 days of its posting), then the White House will have to, and will, respond to it.

Otherwise, there are many, many other things. I again invite you to join us, join the Schiller Institute. Make sure this webcast becomes more known and is spread more widely, because we are in an urgent need for a political discourse: Where should mankind go? How can we organize the world so that it's safe and beautiful for everyone to live in?

Schlanger: That's good advice. I'll second that. Joining the Schiller Institute is an absolutely crucial expression of your own human sentiments. Many of our listeners have joined, but we want to have a big membership drive, and expanding this webcast is one way to do it. So, over the next days, I urge everyone to think of what you can do to make sure this movement advances and succeeds, in bringing the New Silk Road Spirit into every household throughout the trans-Atlantic region, which otherwise is left with nothing but pessimism, depression, and collapse.

Thanks for joining us, Helga. We'll be back next week.

Zepp-LaRouche: Yes, good-bye.

Time To End the Special Relationship; Declassify All British-Spawned Documents Concerning Your 2016 Campaign

by Barbara Boyd

May 24—As of this writing, the U.S. media has its knickers in a complete knot because of "Spygate," the scandal evolving from the President of the United States exercising his constitutional powers to declassify secret intelligence documents bearing on the completely illegal investigation of his 2016 presidential campaign by the Obama White House, Obama's intelligence chiefs, and their masters in the City of London.

In the view of the Anglo-American establishment, Trump is once again being insubordinate, refusing to be told what to do, unlike every American President since the death of FDR, with the exception of John F. Kennedy. So-called "experts" have been trotted out to sniff about "unsubstantiated," "baseless" and "wild" accusations, and "conspiracy theories," propagated by the "unhinged" President of the United States. He aims, they say, to undermine the "rule of law," which, according to them, emanates solely from the personage of Special Counsel Robert Mueller. These experts are taking their cues from former DNI James Clapper and Obama's CIA Chief John Brennan, and include numerous former staffers for Special Counsel Robert Mueller

White House/Shealah Craighead

President Donald Trump. State of the Union Address to Congress, Jan. 30, 2018.

when he was at the FBI, who have become official commentators on CNN and other cable ventures. As we shall show you below, this amounts to letting the future inmates run the institution. They warn how dangerous and illegal the President is being in demanding that the "independent" Justice Department submit to oversight by the Congress, and how dictatorial he has become by asserting that the President of the United States can declassify documents about a coup being run against his Presidency. Turning Abe Lincoln on his head, they seem to think they can fool all the people, all the time.

They bet that people won't pick up and read the Constitution, establishing for themselves that everything President Trump is doing is perfectly and wonderfully legal. The Constitution places the ultimate authority for classifying or declassifying documents, or information, with the President, although in the normal course, that power is delegated to subordinate officials in the Executive branch. The Constitution holds that Congress polices the executive branch agencies, such as the Justice Department, the CIA, and the FBI. These agencies are not independent plenary powers, free to operate however they please. In fact, the Constitution says that Donald Trump is the boss of the DOJ and the intelligence community, no matter how much these agencies may rail against the founding fathers for establishing that fact.

So, the louder these so-called "experts" scream, the more you know you are on to something singularly important and devastating to those responsible for the current ruin of the United States. That something is the fact that Trump is right, and if justice prevails, most of Robert Torquemada Mueller's case is going up in smoke and many of his favored witnesses will be doing time in jail.

A British Operation from the Beginning

We have learned in the past week that the Obama Administration and the British planted a long-time CIA/MI6 asset, Stefan Halper, to run operations against the Trump presidential campaign. As a matter of convenience, it has been claimed that Halper was an FBI informant, since MI6 and the CIA can't legally spy on Americans. But his pedigree is solidly MI6 and CIA, as

we shall see. Revelations to date, point to Halper's role in creating a trail of fake evidence linking the Trump campaign to Russia, in the hopes of derailing Trump's presidential campaign amidst fake charges amounting to treason. The same planted and fake evidence has been picked up and used in Robert Mueller's inquisition against the Trump Presidency. It remains an open question to this writer whether Halper is the Trump campaign "informant" the FBI told British agent Christopher Steele about in the course of the FBI's illicit relationship with Steele—or even the sole informant.

Christopher Steele, of course, is the author of the dirty MI6 dossier claiming that Trump was a Manchurian candidate personally compromised by Vladimir Putin. The British-originated Steele dossier has been a staple for the media and, until recently, the backbone of the entire Russiagate hoax. Steele's dossier was supposedly the "solid" investigative backbone used by the Senate Intelligence Committee in its Russiagate ravings and by the FBI and Justice Department in applying for FISA warrants, and taking other unprecedented steps against an American presidential campaign. Over the past year however, through the dogged investigation of a few brave men in the U.S. House and Senate, Steele's ravings have been exposed as a classic cash-for-trash dirty trick, paid for by Hillary Clinton, but legitimized and spun to the media by the Obama White House, FBI, DOJ, State Department, CIA and DNI. A huge public relations effort involving multiple magazine puff pieces on the British agent, and whole books about his courage and rectitude, did not succeed in vanquishing the fundamental truth exposed by the House Intelligence and Senate Judiciary Committees about Christopher Steele. In the hasty course of doing damage control concerning Steele, a transcript of the testimony of Glenn Simpson before the Senate Judiciary Committee was released, unilaterally, by Senator Dianne Feinstein. In that testimony, Simpson said that the FBI had told Christopher Steele that it had an informant within the Trump campaign. Needless to say, the President and his congressional allies were interested in this unprecedented infiltration, and Stefan Halper has been outed, by the *New York Times* and *Washington Post*, as the informant Steele learned about.

President Trump has displayed extraordinary courage in facing down a hostile intelligence community

and its national media assets which control, for all practical purposes, the majority of the U.S. Congress. "Spygate," and the recent feistiness of the President and his legal team, mean this fight could be a major turning point for the better in U.S. history, provided that the President has popular support and aims at the most vulnerable flank of the operations against him—the illegal British intervention into the U.S. election—in which Stefan Halper and his close friend, Sir Richard Dearlove, were extremely significant players. The dirty Christopher Steele dossier, the operations of the strange Maltese Professor Joseph Mifsud, and Halper's interactions with Trump campaign volunteers Carter Page and George Papadopoulos all emanate from Sir Richard Dearlove's British circle. They preceded by months the official opening of the FBI's "enterprise counterintelligence investigation" and provide the fake evidentiary pretexts to justify that investigation.

The British actors who continue to play the central role in the coup against Donald Trump, hope that all the endless and tantalizing details being dumped about the coup—Michael Cohen, porn star Stormy Daniels, and whatever other barnyard remnants the "Resistance" is able to throw at the American people—will combine with the anti-Russian blind spot of U.S. congressional investigators to bury the truth, the actual story here. The actual story, which we explore below, is that the British and their friends in the Obama Administration ran an information warfare operation against the American presidential campaign of Donald Trump, because *they knew that Trump could win* the election against Hillary Clinton, an uninspiring robot candidate who had completely lost touch with any Americans not associated with the bi-coastal elites. They violated numerous U.S. laws in the process.

As Lyndon LaRouche has repeatedly insisted, this was an international operation, not something confined to the United States. The British establishment—in shock over the popular revolt represented in the Brexit vote, finding similar dissent throughout their European colonies, being outflanked by Putin in Syria and Ukraine, viewing China's Belt and Road Initiative as a deadly strategic threat, and sitting on top of a hopeless speculative financial powder keg—faced the danger, if Clinton lost, of losing the United States as their designated gendarme for the world.

They panicked. As MI6's Christopher Steele con-

Gage Skidmore

Uninspiring robot candidate Hillary Clinton speaking to supporters, January 2016.

White House/flikr

CIA Director Brennan speaking with President Obama.

fessed to former DOJ Associate Deputy Attorney General Bruce Ohr, he and his friends across the pond were "desperate to stop Trump's election." They launched a furious operation to destroy Donald Trump because of Trump's determination to seek a new, collaborative relationship with Putin and Russia, and because of Trump's pledge to end the U.S. role as world policeman. They found willing collaborators in the Obama and Clinton partisans manning the Department of Justice and Obama's intelligence agencies, and in their longstanding assets in the United States. According to George Neumayr's explosive report in the *American Spectator* of May 22, John Brennan said his extraordinary and completely illegal convening of an inter-agency task force at CIA headquarters to attack the Trump campaign in the early spring of 2016 was the result of Trump putting *"the special relationship"* with the British at risk. After assuming the Presidency, Trump refused to back down on his quest for better relations with Russia, despite everything they have thrown at him. In addition, he formed a personal friendship with China's Xi Jinping. As a result, Perfidious Albion has doubled down on its machinations. It has acted to continue the coup while engaging in provocations and false flag operations against Russia, such as the Skripal poisoning hoax and the bogus claim that Assad used chemical weapons against Syria's citizens. They seek to corner Trump into obedience, to cause his impeachment, or both.

The President seems to have focused his initial attention on getting certain documents at the FBI and Department of Justice declassified. He shouldn't expect to find the story about this British operation in the files of the DOJ or FBI, however—they just got the manufactured

public domain/Domusrulez

Sir Richard Dearlove, former head of MI6.

UK Government

Robert Hannigan, former director of GCHQ. Key figure in "Spygate" being run against President Trump.

Facebook/Natalia Veselnitskaya

Natalia Veselnitskaya, Russian lawyer.

end-products. Whole chunks of information about this operation exist only in the files and recorded interactions of the Obama White House, Obama's CIA, DNI, Treasury Department, and State Department, as well as of the British old-boy spy networks and "private" spy companies affiliated with Sir Richard Dearlove, and the official British spy agencies—MI6 and GCHQ. Senator Rand Paul has taken the right approach by forcing this issue with the new head of the CIA, Gina Haspel. Senator Paul has demanded to know what Haspel knows about the British/U.S. spy operations against the President. Haspel, a devotee of MI6, a Russia hater, and an acolyte of John Brennan, was the CIA station chief in London during the entire 2014-2017 time period, and, thus, either a key player in these operations or someone who knows a whole lot about them.

Kimberley Strassel at the *Wall Street Journal* has repeatedly called for the President to use his power to declassify the documents which the Justice Department and the intelligence agencies are yelping about and withholding. Strassel is absolutely correct, but the declassification process has to be much larger. In our view, the relevant documents in U.S. agencies to be targeted for declassification include the following:

(1) all the documents referencing the allegations fed by the British, NATO allies, Ukraine, or Estonia, to U.S. agencies concerning the Trump campaign's alleged connections to Russia, beginning no later than 2015, if not earlier;

(2) all documents referencing the claim that Trump was a Manchurian candidate, a Putin puppet, as circulated through the Clinton campaign, the news media, and the Obama White House, State Department, CIA and FBI;

(3) all documents concerning the summer 2016 face-to-face meeting between John Brennan and GCHQ Director Robert Hannigan;

(4) all documents referencing British knowledge of an alleged Russian hack of the Democratic National Committee's computers dating from 2015 or earlier; all documents in which the CIA's "Marble Framework" was used to falsely attribute cyberattacks to nation states; all documents pertaining to *Wikileaks*' acquisition of the DNC and Podesta emails; and all documents pertaining to former NSA Technical Director Bill Binney's meeting with Mike Pompeo concerning the alleged DNC/Podesta hacks;

(5) all documents concerning surveillance and counterintelligence tools deployed against the Trump campaign and transition as the result of Executive Order 12333 or other classified techniques; and

(6) all documents concerning entrapment and infiltration exercises conducted against the campaign, including, specifically, all State Department and intelligence agency documents concerning the June 2016 Trump Tower meeting with Russian lawyer Natalia Veselnitskaya.

These documents, and all the documents presently under subpoena or otherwise requested by the House Intelligence Committee, House Judiciary Committee, House Government Affairs Committee, and the Senate Judiciary Committee related to the Trump/Russia investigation, should be declassified now and shared with the American public.

To complete the picture, the President should also demand that the British provide him with all information from their side of the pond, concerning the role of British intelligence services or British intelligence-related operatives in attempting to discredit both himself and Vladimir Putin in the operation popularly known as "Russiagate," an operation which continues to the present day on both sides of the Atlantic and throughout Europe. While the President's allies in the Congress have proved to be terrific and courageous investigators, they are blinded by years of British brainwashing and partisan legends about Putin and Russia. They are attempting to sell the fake story that the Russians manipulated the elections but did so only benefit to Hillary Clinton or to sow "divisiveness" in an already deeply polarized and divided American public.

If the Brits don't fess up and cooperate, then sanction them in a targeted fashion, starting with the City of London financial center, the heart of the new British Empire. This is the swamp which must be drained, the actual parasite now sucking the life out of the U.S. economy: the City of London, its offshore hot money financial havens, together with its American dupes and appendages. This is the swamp which would engage us in new and deadly wars targeted at both Russia and China. It is the center of the war being waged against the United States and its new President.

Birth of the FBI Investigation of Trump: An Ever-Shifting Story

Steele Dossier Blows Up with Multiple Casualties

Stefan Halper's role in the coup against the President emerged as the House Intelligence Committee dug deep in order to figure out exactly how the unprecedented and illegal FBI counterintelligence investigation against the Trump campaign began. Initially, following leads from leaks to the news media by the intelligence community and Democrats, and their own investigation, House Republicans focused on Steele's dirty dossier as the probable point of origin. That focus produced major scandals as House investigators discovered that the dirty, anonymously sourced, third-party-hearsay hit job against the Trump campaign, parading as an intelligence product from the man who headed MI6's Russia desk, turned out to have been paid for by Hillary Clinton; pumped by the likes of John Brennan, James Clapper, and the Clinton campaign to publicly Putin-bait Trump throughout the last weeks of the Presidential campaign; and used by Clapper and James Comey in a blatant attempt to intimidate the President-elect in a January 6, 2017 meeting at Trump Tower. At that meeting, Comey confronted the President with Steele's fake claims, correctly referencing the experience as akin to his "J. Edgar Hoover" moment. James Clapper had previously leaked the contents of the dirty dossier to CNN. Comey told Trump he was telling him about Steele's dubious dirt because CNN already had the dirty document and was about to publish it. Of course, Comey left out the fact that CNN only had the document because Clapper had leaked it to them. In addition, David Kramer, John McCain's longtime aide, had the dirty document, having received it via British intelligence's Sir Andrew Wood, a high level associate in Steele's firm, Orbis Business Intelligence, and from Christopher Steele, personally. Kramer leaked it to *Buzzfeed*. When Trump stood his ground and demanded that Comey investigate the source of the fake allegations, *Buzzfeed* published the British dirt, smearing the incoming President of the United States as a sexual pervert who had been compromised by Putin.

After almost two years of FBI investigation, Steele's main claims either could not be verified or stood refuted. But against its own guidelines, in the Fall of 2016, the FBI used the unverified Steele Dossier to procure a FISA warrant on Carter Page, never telling the Court that the Clinton campaign had paid for Steele's hit job and that Steele himself had been terminated by the FBI because he lied about his contacts with the news media. This warrant was obtained and continued even after the Fall 2016 departure of Carter Page from the Trump Campaign. And it was, reportedly, preceded by FISA warrants in which Page was a subject, dating back to 2014. In other words, Carter Page, one of many weird members of Donald Trump's Foreign Policy Advisory Board, was a walking government microphone. Prior to formally terminating its relationship to Christopher Steele in October of 2016, the FBI told the British agent something which, under relevant guidelines, should never have been disclosed to a foreign agent: that they had an informant in the Trump Campaign. After his termination, Steele continued to feed his information into the coup plotters through a different official channel, Bruce Ohr, the former Associate Deputy Attorney General of the United States. Ohr's wife Nellie worked for Steele's American employer, Fusion GPS. As a result of the Ohr/Steele relationship coming to light, Ohr was demoted. Senator Chuck Grassley continues to demand

CC/Rich Girard

James Comey, former FBI Director.

Creative Commons/MSNBC

Carter Page, former foreign policy advisor to Trump campaign.

Ohr's testimony and is pursuing other avenues concerning Steele's actions.

True to the clandestine nature of this entire affair, the Steele dossier was not delivered to the FBI by normal law enforcement or intelligence channels. Rather, it arrived by way of the very partisan U.S. State Department, formerly led by Hillary Clinton. Steele had previously provided more than a hundred memos to assist Victoria Nuland in her role as U.S. case officer for the British-inspired 2014 regime-change operation in Ukraine. Nuland authorized the initial July 2016 meeting between Steele and Michael Gaeta, the former FBI Eurasian organized crime task force member who had worked previously with Steele and was now stationed in Rome. Gaeta reported Steele's bogus claims about Trump and Russia to FBI headquarters. At the same time, Steele's friend at State, Secretary Kerry's long-time counsel, Jonathan Winer, vouched for Steele and put him in touch with Clinton operatives Sidney Blumenthal and Cody Shearer, who made similar bogus claims about Trump and Russia. Steele used the Blumenthal/Shearer charges to corroborate his own wild charges to the FBI. At the center of the initial Steele memos was the July 2016 trip to Moscow by Carter Page. As we shall see below, Stefan Halper struck up a relationship with Page almost as soon as Page stepped off the plane from Moscow in London, in July of 2016. This relationship continued, involving numerous meetings and correspondence, until September of 2017.

Based on the exposures by the House Intelligence Committee, and Steele's referral for criminal prosecution by Senators Chuck Grassley and Lindsey Graham, the Steele dossier has become a political hot potato in the ongoing narrative promulgated by the coup-meisters. Their current *diktat* is that it is to be referenced only as part of a larger mosaic which can somehow, when taken altogether, legitimize the unprecedented FBI investigation of the Republican presidential nominee. In the meantime, Tom Steyer and other Democratic Party, Silicon Valley billionaires have provided over $50 million to Fusion GPS and Steele's British company in an all-out effort, led by Senator Dianne Feinstein's former staffer, Daniel Jones, to somehow resuscitate the Steele dossier's bogus and discredited claims.

Alexander Downer, Australian Ambassador to UK. Key figure in 2016 attempted Russiagate against President Trump.

Narrative #2: Papadopoulos Did It

With Steele's British tale embroiled in scandal, a new official narrative has been ginned up and provided to the Congress and the news media. This narrative says that George Papadopoulos' drunken claims to the Australian High Commissioner in London, Alexander Downer, at a high-class London bar, provoked the FBI's investigation of Trump. It presents Papadopoulos' interactions with the Australian, Downer; the Steele dossier; and, now, the spy Halper's interactions with Papadopoulos and Carter Page; and the alleged Russian hack of the DNC, as if they were all separate events, rather than just aspects of the same large British operation to fabricate a pretext for the FBI to investigate Trump.

According to this narrative, the drunken Papadopoulos, stalked and courted by Downer, mouthed off to the Australian diplomat in May 2016, that he knew that the Russians had thousands of Hillary Clinton's emails. Downer reported this to the Australian government which then reported it to the FBI after the June 15, 2016 attribution of the "DNC hack" to the Russians by CrowdStrike and the July publication of the DNC emails by *Wikileaks.* CrowdStrike was paid for its attribution services by the

George Papadopoulos, young Trump campaign staffer stalked by Ambassador Downer.

same Democratic Party law firm which was paying Christopher Steele. This new narrative, however, has multiple problems, in addition to the fact that it is incredible on its face. The biggest problem is that when it is followed through, it exposes the months of CIA and MI6 illicit activities preceding the official opening of the formal FBI counterintelligence investigation in July of 2016.

We now know, as the result of the recent declassification of the FBI's Memo originating the investigation, that Papadopoulos, Carter Page, Michael Flynn, and Paul Manafort were the immediate targets of the FBI/Trump counterintelligence probe—code-named "Crossfire Hurricane"—and formally opened in July of 2016. Not to make too much of it, but the FBI didn't even use an American name to disguise this British-originated operation and the manufactured evidence which accompanied it into FBI files, instead adopting a line from the Rolling Stones' "Jumpin Jack Flash" as the investigation's moniker.

It is claimed that Papadopoulos learned about Russian possession of Clinton's emails, about six weeks after the 28-year-old ingenue inserted himself into the clumsily and hastily formed Trump Foreign Policy Advisory team in early March 2016. He learned this from a mysterious Maltese professor, Joseph Mifsud, who, according to Robert Mueller, had to be a Russian intelligence agent targeting Papadopoulos. Throughout March and April of 2016, Mifsud courted Papadopoulos, giving him a job, introducing him to someone he falsely claimed was Putin's niece, introducing young George Papadopoulos to Ivan Timofeev of the Russian International Affairs Council, and claiming to George in a meeting on April 26, that he has just met with high level Russian government officials in Moscow who had "dirt" on Clinton in the form of thousands of her emails. Papadopoulos eagerly passed this information on to Trump Campaign officials in the form of written emails and public Facebook chats, while constantly seeking to set up meetings with high level Russian agents he believed he could broker. His offers were refused, but a huge document cache was fabricated, providing the pretext for further investigation. As we will further detail below, it now appears that Mifsud was also a British intelligence operative.

On July 7, 2016, Carter Page traveled to Moscow to give a speech at the New Economic School. He flew to London immediately after, where he met Stefan Halper at a Cambridge University event about the 2016 U.S. elections, and continued to communicate with Halper through September of 2017. Christopher Steele was at the same event, positioning himself, according to some accounts, right behind Page. Page's July Moscow trip forms a major part of Christopher Steele's first memos concerning Russian contacts with the Trump Campaign. Steele claimed, absurdly, that Carter Page had been offered a major share in the Russian state oil company, Gazprom, if he could broker the ending of the Magnitsky Act sanctions on Russia.

In between the courtship of Papadopoulos and the Page meeting, another set-up meeting to feed the growing FBI fake file, occurred at Trump Tower in New York City on June 16, 2016. As we detail below, a British publicist, Rob Goldstone, wrote to Donald Trump, Jr. to set up a meeting with a Russian lawyer who would deliver "dirt" on Hillary Clinton straight from the "Crown Prosecutor of Russia." Although nothing like that actually occurred at the meeting, the fake evidence trail had been created for future prosecutive purposes. This meeting was exploited by another high-level British intelligence agent, Bill Browder, who formally complained to the Justice Department that participants in the meeting had violated the Foreign Agents Registration Act. Eleven days after the Trump Tower meeting, Christopher Steele wrote his first memo noting that the Russians and the Trump campaign were in contact,

CC/Hudson Institute

Bill Browder, high-level British intelligence agent.

developing "dirt" about Hillary Clinton in a well-designed collusion operation.

In September of 2016, Stefan Halper, out of the blue, offered $3,000 to George Papadopoulos to write a paper about oil fields in the Mediterranean. Papadopoulos went to London, met Halper, and was aggressively queried by him about his knowledge of Russian hacks of "the emails," circling back on the fake facts presented by the Maltese professor. Papadopoulos allegedly said he didn't know what Halper was talking about, much to Halper's chagrin. According to some accounts, Halper also used a sexy assistant to try and enmesh boy George further in his sway. He met with Papadopoulos on multiple occasions following this introduction. At the same time, Halper met with Sam Clovis, who chaired the Trump Foreign Intelligence Advisory Board, and sought a formal position in the Trump campaign.

As revealed in the media to date, Stefan Halper, while still operating on or through Carter Page and Papadopoulos, on behalf of the FBI, the CIA and MI6 against the Trump campaign and the incoming Administration, sought an ambassadorship in the Trump Administration, reportedly in an Asian country. He used Peter Navarro, Trump's anti-China trade assistant, as his emissary.

The Inconvenient Facts of the Matter

The claim that the FBI initiated an unprecedented investigation of the Republican Presidential nominee based on a drunken and very ambiguous conversation with George Papadopoulos about Hillary Clinton's emails, is ridiculous. It is backpedaling, revisionist history and never happened. Hillary Clinton erased 30,000 emails from her illicit and unsecure basement server, and it was assumed by many that the Russians (and potentially other hackers) had them. They were eagerly sought by the Republicans in pursuit of their claim that Clinton engaged in illegal activities and compromised classified information through her use of her email private server. It is simply beyond a stretch to insinuate that Mifsud and boy George were privy to British intelligence information, allegedly passed to the United States in 2015, that the Russians had hacked the DNC, or that the Russians would confess their dirty deed to the likes of Joseph Mifsud.

Moreover, the Russian hack of the DNC and 2016 handover of files to *Wikileaks* never happened. On a simple level, the very clumsy official narrative instructs us that the Russians were inside the DNC's computers as of 2015, the DNC was warned about it by the FBI, and yet nothing, absolutely nothing, was done about this. The tip that the Russians were inside the DNC computers, of course, came from the British. William Binney, a former technical director of the NSA, points out that the NSA monitors all Internet activity throughout the world and would be able to document and demonstrate the alleged Russian hack and any Internet transmission of DNC files to *Wikileaks*, if, indeed, either event ever happened. No such document has been provided. Rather, the American public was told to rely on "assessments" from intelligence analysts hand-picked by John Brennan, for the assertion that the Russians hacked the DNC and John Podesta, and gave the product to *Wikileaks*. When confronted about this evidence-free "assessment," Brennan simply states that he "does not do evidence."

Binney and others have demonstrated that the DNC files which ultimately ended up at *Wikileaks* derived from an internal leak, not a Russian hack, just as *Wikileaks* has consistently asserted. (See https://www.thenation.com/article/a-new-report-raises-big-questions-about-last-years-dnc-hack/ and https://www.larouchepub.com/other/2017/4430_vips_expose_rus-gate.html) It is noteworthy that the CIA's "Marble Framework" allows the CIA to create false-flag cyberattacks by leaving behind false signatures of behavior in order to attribute cyberattacks to other countries. The FBI never did any forensic analysis of the DNC's computers. Instead they simply accepted the analysis of CrowdStrike's Alperovitch, a Russian-born, anti-Putin fanatic who, aside from being paid by the DNC, associated himself with the Atlantic Council's

Institute of Politics/Kristyn Ulanday

Michael Flynn, former Director of Defense Intelligence Agency, was also a target of the FBI counterintelligence probe of Trump.

Digital Research Lab. The Lab itself is incorporated into NATO's Centre for Strategic Communications, a British operation which has been conducting cyberwar against Russia and "exposes" about alleged Russian disinformation activities since the 2014 coup in Ukraine.

Andrew McCarthy, Kimberley Strassel, and Byron York have all noted that the final House Intelligence Report on Russian Interference in the 2016 Election states that James Comey briefed the principals of the National Security Council "on the Page information," in "late Spring of 2016." The principals were the highest ranking national security officials of the Obama Administration. Apparently, according to the same report, shortly before the Obama White House principals' meeting, James Comey, Andrew McCabe, and Loretta Lynch all met. The subject was the same: Carter Page. The Democratic version of the House Report states that the FBI interviewed Carter Page in March 2016. Page had previously collaborated with the FBI in 2013 in the prosecution of Russians operatives who allegedly targeted Page for recruitment while referring to him constantly as an "idiot." Most U.S. media accounts of Page's activities, including those of the President's supporters, echo the alleged Russian sentiment. The friendliest accounts call him an "eccentric" and a "knucklehead." From the moment he insinuated himself into Trump's Foreign Policy Advisory team, in March of 2016, Page began a public speaking campaign strongly supporting Putin and Russia while denouncing the United States.

Michael Flynn joined the Trump campaign as an advisor in February 2016. Paul Manafort joined the campaign to manage convention operations in March and was named campaign manager in May. Both were hated by the Obama White House and the British: Manafort for his activities on behalf of the duly elected President of Ukraine, Viktor Yanukovych, whom the British and Americans deposed in 2014, and Flynn for exposing Obama Administration direct support of terrorists in Syria, while also seeking better relations with Russia's Putin in order to deal with international terrorism. According to the BBC and other sources, in the early spring of 2016, no later than March, John Brennan had convened his completely illegal inter-agency task force at CIA headquarters operating off of "British tips" about Trump and Russia and targeting the Trump campaign.

Some time in the summer of 2016, GCHQ's Robert Hannigan flew to Washington to deliver some type of product to Brennan personally. Hannigan resigned, unexpectedly, following the U.S. election. It is possible that Hannigan was providing the intercepted communications between the patsies, Papadopoulos and Page, and their Russian and Trump campaign interlocutors. Most informed observers believe that Hannigan's resignation was a late British effort to dissociate the government itself from the election operations against Trump. For those who might not know it, it is completely illegal for the CIA to spy on American citizens, let alone an American presidential campaign, or to farm out that activity to foreign intelligence agencies.

All of what we have said here derives from the House Intelligence Committee reports, court documents, and well-informed reporting. It plainly shows that the British used the Obama CIA and DNI and a bevy of their own agents, to create the fake basis for the FBI "Crossfire Hurricane" investigation of Donald Trump, Michael Flynn and Paul Manafort. Page and Papadopoulos were at least used as plants for fake and false allegations, if they were not, themselves, compromised as informants.

The People Across the Pond: Looking Behind the Curtain

Sir Richard Dearlove, KCMG, OBE, was Christopher Steele's boss as head of MI6 from 1999 to 2004. Steele and his business partner, Christopher Burrows, remain extremely close to Dearlove. By their own accounts, Sir Richard mentored and shepherded their calculated information warfare operation against the Trump campaign. A major force in the U.S./British anti-Russian Henry Jackson Society of neo-conservatives, Sir Richard is widely blamed, correctly, for the

Chris Burrows, Christopher Steele's business partner at Orbis Business Intelligence, Ltd.

fake intelligence which led the United States into the disastrous Iraq War. Christopher Steele's private intelligence firm, Orbis Business Intelligence, makes a great deal of money, according to Steele's own account, providing "intelligence" to warring Russian oligarchs, the perfect cover for disruption and low intensity warfare operations against the modern Russian state.

Stefan Halper, the son-in-law of the CIA's Ray Cline by his first marriage, has a long history with the CIA and the Bush family. In the 1980 presidential campaign, Halper worked with a team of CIA agents promoting the candidacy of George H.W. Bush. After the Republican primaries, Halper was accused of pilfering certain documents from the Carter campaign, disclosing how Carter would deal with Ronald Reagan in the general election. You would think that MI6 could come up with someone new to run intelligence agency operations in elections, rather than an aging veteran of the trade. Later, Halper chaired Palmer Bank, which is where Oliver North laundered money destined for the illegal Contra insurgency operation. From 2001 through 2015, Halper taught international affairs and American studies at Cambridge. In the British intelligence trade, universities are prime grounds both for recruitment and for spying operations. Halper and Dearlove have been described as very close friends, and together chaired, for years, the Cambridge Security Initiative, which featured policy talks involving spooks from throughout the world. From 2012 forward, Halper earned more than a million dollars working on contracts with the Pentagon's Office of Net Assessment, the spook domain formerly chaired by the utopian Andrew Marshall. His chief engagement there appears to have been in producing multiple studies bashing China.

Alexander Downer, Halper, and Dearlove share deep connections to another British private intelligence firm, Hakluyt & Company, described frequently as the favorite retirement home for premier MI6 spies. Richard Hakluyt was a 16th century geographer who is described as a principal inspiration for the formation of the infamous British East India Company. This private company, not the British government, was the heart of the British Empire. Downer was on the advisory board of Hakluyt. He has also been associated, in his role as a diplomat for Australia, with a $25 million grant to the Clinton Foundation to fight AIDS. Dearlove is personally close to Hakluyt's founder, Mike Reynolds, the former head of station in Germany for MI6. Stefan Halper has co-authored two books with Hakluyt's Jonathan Clarke.

This group's targeting of Michael Flynn dates from Flynn's attendance at a Cambridge Intelligence Seminar in February of 2014, while he was still director of the DIA, if not earlier. According to the *Daily Caller's* Chuck Ross, who has provided the best reporting on Halper's activities, Halper falsely claimed that Flynn had been compromised by a Russian woman at the Seminar, Svetlana Lokhova, and reported this bogus claim to U.S. authorities while circulating it in the U.S. and British news media. Lokhova is still a teacher and researcher at Cambridge, and Halper's claims were found to be baseless. This dovetails with the focus on Flynn in Luke Harding's book, *Collusion*, which attempts to salvage Christopher Steele's reputation. Harding, MI6's favorite reporter, details extensive British intelligence reporting and investigation of Flynn based on the simple fact that he visited the headquarters of the GRU in Russia in an official capacity. Many believe that Flynn's firing by the Obama Administration was based on British complaints.

Halper and Dearlove resigned as conveners of the Cambridge Security Initiative in December of 2016, claiming that it had been infiltrated by the Russians. According to other MI6-related leaders of the seminar series, this charge also was completely bogus. As of 2018, Dearlove has resumed his association with the Cambridge intelligence seminars, and Svetlana Lokhova is listed as a speaker for a program on May 18,

C-SPAN screen shot

Stefan Halper, long-time CIA/MI6 asset. Planted by the Obama Administration and the British to run operations against the Trump campaign.

2018. Such are the ways of British intelligence operations.

The capper in this spy story so far, though, is that the strange Maltese professor who provided the fake Russian dirt concerning Hillary Clinton's emails to Papadopoulos, also appears to be a British intelligence operative. Numerous reports link Mifsud to Claire Smith, a major figure in the upper echelons of British intelligence who vets all UK intelligence personnel. Mifsud has disappeared off the face of the earth since his doings were exposed. In a statement to the Italian press, before his disappearance, he denied being a Russian operative and stated that he was a member of the European Council on Foreign Relations and the Clinton Foundation.

The June 2016 Trump Tower Meeting: Time for Another Look

No examination of British operations against the Trump campaign would be complete without revisiting the meeting on June 9, 2016, involving Jared Kushner, Paul Manafort, Donald Trump, Jr., and five other people, only one of whom was Russian—the lawyer Natalia Veselnitskaya. By all accounts provided by participants, the meeting was very short, and involved the Magnitsky Act sanctions imposed by the U.S. Congress on certain Russians. These were, of course, the same sanctions referenced by Christopher Steele in his bogus claim that Carter Page was involved in a bribe involving Gazprom shares and rolling back the sanctions.

The emails setting up the meeting do not reflect what actually happened. These emails, written by British publicist Rob Goldstone, purport to offer dirt, straight from the "Russian Crown Prosecutor," about Hillary Clinton, for use by Trump, along with further offers of help directly from the Russian government. Right after creating this very crude fake file, Goldstone disappeared on what appeared to be a world-wide tour of gay bathhouses, only to turn up significantly later. The document-trail for future use was created and there was no need to stick around. Can anyone be blind to the pattern here?

On July 15, 2016, just before the FBI opened its "Crossfire Hurricane" charade, Bill Browder filed a complaint with the U.S. Department of Justice concerning four participants in the Trump Tower meeting and others for failure to register under the Foreign Agents Registration Act. Browder's complaint claimed that Veselnitskaya's contingent at the Trump Tower meeting, none of whom were Russians, were engaged in unregistered Russian lobbying activities, namely, attempting to overturn the Magnitsky Act. Browder, the grandson of the former head of the Communist Party U.S.A., renounced his American citizenship in 1989 to become a British subject and has since operated at the highest levels of British intelligence. His Magnitsky Act sanctions were the brainchild of Jonathan Winer, previously referenced in this spy saga for his role in laundering the Christopher Steele dossier to the FBI. Browder, Winer, and Steele have had a years-long "close friendship" according to statements made by Winer.

According to *Foreign Policy* magazine and others, on July 11, 2017, a hacker going by the name of "Johnnie Walker" published a trove of emails from the private account of Lieutenant Robert J. Otto, who is tasked to a secretive unit in the U.S. State Department focused on Russia. *Newsweek* magazine states that Otto is the nation's "foremost" intelligence guy concerning Russia. The emails have not been authenticated. However, they include an email purported to have been written on the day of the Trump Tower meeting between Otto and Kyle Parker, of the House Committee on Foreign Affairs, featuring a picture of Russian attorney Natalia Velselnitskaya's house in Russia. Parker credits himself as the actual author of the Magnitsky Act sanctions against Russia, and is a close friend of Bill Browder. Velselnitskaya claims that her children have been threatened as a result of her participation in a legal case questioning the *bona fides* of Bill Browder and the factual foundations of the Magnitsky Act. The picture of her house in this context suggests another level of intense surveillance directed at Trump Tower on the day of the meeting, and the possibility that threats to her family were actually governing Veselnitskaya's behavior. Strangely, Veselnitskaya was in the United States based on a State Department visa granted over strident U.S. Department of Justice opposition.

As we noted previously, Christopher Steele's first memo in his dirty dossier was written 11 days after the June 15, 2016 Trump Tower meeting and alleged that the Russians were providing the Trump Campaign with negative information about Clinton as part of a well-crafted collusion scheme.

We are told that President Trump is a target of Special Counsel Mueller regarding this meeting because he provided "false exculpatory" information to counter media accounts which originally portrayed the Trump Tower meeting as a smoking gun in the Trump/Russia collusion saga. As the President has otherwise correctly characterized Mueller's obstruction-of-justice fantasies, the special prosecutor seeks to criminalize the simple act of fighting back against a frame-up which Mueller must know by now, was orchestrated by the British and the Obama Administration. Based on this writer's experience with Mueller in the prosecution of Lyndon LaRouche, however, it is probable that our own Torquemada was in on the game from the day he was appointed.

A Personal Post-Script

This very British tale of fabricating and planting evidence may seem foreign to what anyone learned in civics class about the American legal system. Here is an anecdote from the Boston prosecution of Lyndon LaRouche, supervised by Robert Mueller, for you to ponder. Through extensive surveillance and infiltration during the two years prior to the Boston indictments of LaRouche and his associates, the prosecutors in the LaRouche case knew that some of the LaRouche defendants in that case recorded all significant conversations in their notebooks for future reporting purposes. Mueller's lead prosecutor, John Markham, tasked an FBI informant, Ryan Quade Emerson, to suggest that the defendants obstruct justice, and Emerson's remarks were duly recorded in the notebooks. Markham then used the fabricated notebook entries, in his opening statement to the jury, as proof that the LaRouche defendants intended to obstruct justice, without disclosing the fact that he authored those comments or that he laundered them through an FBI informant into the notebooks. U.S. District Judge Robert Keeton, reflecting the judicial norms of previous times, found in that case that Mueller, Markham, and their DOJ supervisors engaged in systemic, institutional, prosecutorial misconduct.

Developments in Italy Offer Chance for a Reorganization in Europe

by Helga Zepp-LaRouche, chairwoman of the German political party Civil Rights Movement Solidarity (*BüSo*)

Written one day before the EU blocked Italy's popularly-elected government.

May 26—It is no coincidence that the reactions to the proposed new government in Italy from neo-liberal circles are as hysterical as the reactions to Trump's election victory were. There are two options now: financial warfare, as some suggest, and thus the end of the euro and the EU, with the risk of developments occurring such as those during the 1920s and 30s; or the positive, programmatic approaches in the coalition agreement of the Lega and Five-Star Movement—such as the Glass-Steagall Act and a national investment bank—to carry out the already urgent reorganization of the trans-Atlantic financial system.

In an astonishing combination of arrogance and economic misunderstanding, politicians and media representatives have threatened to put Italy on a tight rein from Brussels (Claus Kleber on *ZDF*); suggested that the new government was on a "suicide mission" (*Spiegel*); that "the putative government's legislative program would plunge the

country into insolvency so quickly that it is widely regarded as a joke" (*London Times*); that Italy has its proverbial *dolce far niente* ["idle sweetness"] financed by others, which is "aggressive freeloading" (Jan Fleischauer in *Spiegel*); or—in an undisguised threat of financial warfare—"If necessary, the financial markets would put them back on the path of virtue" (Daniel Caspary, Chairman of the CDU-CSU group in the European Parliament); "A storm is brewing," no solidarity with Italy if it changes course (Elmar Brok); or, "a government program for the document shredder" (*Deutschlandfunk*).

It is food for thought when circles that normally can't stop harping on the alleged lack of democracy in China, have no problem deriding the electoral decision of an EU member state.

These representatives of the neo-liberal establishment are obviously as incapable as Hillary Clinton of reflecting on the reasons why voters reject a policy they see as an attack on their standard of living and their prospects for the future. The revolt against this policy (which serves the interests of banks and speculators)

Italy's new Prime Minister, Giuseppe Conte (left), whose choice of Paolo Savona (above), a newly staunch opponent of the euro, created a furor in the EU and the big-bank establishment.

Giuseppe Conte facebook page

has continued since Brexit in a series of similar voting results: the electoral victory of Donald Trump, the "No" vote on the constitutional amendment in Italy, the election in Austria, and just now the election in Italy.

The reason that two Euroskeptical parties won there is obvious. The experience that Italy has had with the austerity policy imposed by Brussels and former German Finance Minister Wolfgang Schäuble has been negative. Thanks to compliance with the Maastricht criteria, the Italian economy went from growth to stagnation and then sank into recession. Actual unemployment is around 20%, and youth unemployment in the South is 60%. More than 250,000 Italians emigrate per year, which obviously represents a massive weakening of economic potential, and the health care system has deteriorated massively.

In addition, Italy feels totally abandoned by the EU on the refugee issue. Over the years Italy has been a prize pupil of the EU, achieving a steady primary surplus and a balanced or even positive trade and payments balance, but nevertheless economic output has fallen since the introduction of the euro. Thanks to the budgetary discipline required by the EU, the average income has fallen behind that of Spain and industrial production is 20% below that of 2008. This "discipline" has also widened the gap between the industrialized North and the less developed South.

The best example of the change in sentiment towards the EU and the European Monetary Union is economist Paolo Savona, who went from being pro-Euro to a staunch opponent when he saw the consequences for Italian economy and society. Savona, who was a banker and a minister in previous governments, proposed a "Plan B" if staying in the euro proved to be too painful for Italy. He also described the euro as a "German prison" for Italy. The *Manager-Magazin* described him as a "true Eurofright."

But much more appropriately, the former chairman of the Italian metalworkers union, Giorgio Cremaschi, sent out a tweet, commenting: "The fact that a moderate like Paolo Savona, a supporter of La Malfa and a minister in the Ciampi government, is today considered a public enemy of the EU & Co., is a sign of how far to the right the policy has drifted in Italy and Europe, after decades of neo-liberal policies by center-left and center-right governments."

A Crash of 'Biblical Proportions'

The truth is, that in the case of Greece or of Italy, it was never about saving those countries—it was always about the banks. It is interesting to note that the first initiative of the new Prime Minister Conte was to meet with the victims of the bail-in operations which the EU had ordered earlier Prime Ministers Renzi and Gentiloni to undertake against small savers in banks and savings banks in Tuscany and the Veneto region. Conte promised them that they would be entitled to protection for their savings, which often took a lifetime of work to accumulate, and which are guaranteed by the constitution. Those who were betrayed or deceived, he said, would be compensated.

While the neo-liberal protagonists are working themselves up about Italy, we should instead be glad that there is an important government in Europe that is considering solutions to the looming financial crisis. Because the next crash could happen at any time and tear down the foundations of our societies. The business blog, *Mauldin Economics*. joined those sounding the alarm, speaking of a new financial crash of "biblical proportions" in view of the enormously increased debt, especially corporate debt.

Perhaps it would be a good thing for the parties in Germany who have a "C" for "Christian" in their names, to pay heed to the recent paper of the Vatican Congregation for the Doctrine of the Faith, which warns that the banks' derivative transactions are a "ticking time bomb,"and that the current financial system is totally unacceptable, both economically and morally. Another aspect was emphasized by President Putin in his speech to the St. Petersburg International Economic Forum, where he warned against the effects of sanctions and the unilateral break with previously accepted rules [by the U.S. Senate]. This could trigger a systemic crisis that the world has never seen, he warned, or at least not for a long time.

Perhaps the turmoil and changes at the Deutsche Bank are an indication of the realization among some of those responsible, that the neo-liberal course was the wrong track. Two years ago, Lyndon LaRouche demanded that the German bank return to the tradition of former chairman Alfred Herrhausen, and its reducing its investment banking business today is definitely a step in the right direction. But the clock is ticking. The social protests in France should be a warning that people no longer want to accept policies that favor the speculators.

The Alternative

What is needed is the full program proposed by Lyndon LaRouche in the "Four Laws": in capsule summary, a banking separation law in the tradition of Glass-Steagall, a National Bank for investment in the real economy, an international credit system, and a massive increase in economic productivity through crash programs for nuclear fusion and international space cooperation.

Even if it is difficult to imagine where such a reorganization should come from in Europe, given the prevailing ideologies in Brussels and, unfortunately, Berlin, it is existential. President Trump has repeatedly promised to reintroduce the Glass-Steagall Act and Alexander Hamilton's American System of economics. As the turmoil surrounding the Italian government's program is sure to increase, this will provide the opportunity to put a reorganization of the hopelessly bankrupt transatlantic financial system on the agenda—provided that there are enough citizens who

Presidential website/Tass

Russian President Vladimir Putin, addressing the 22nd St. Petersburg International Economic Forum, May 25, 2018.

support the efforts of the BüSo party and the Schiller Institute.

Another aspect, which has a lot to do with the issue being addressed here, is the fact that China is in the process of completely transforming its population policy. Chinese media report that the previous demographic policy of allowing only one, and then two children per family is now considered completely wrong. This policy was formulated under the impression that there are only limited resources, so that every additional person is a burden. However, this has given way to the realization that every additional child represents an enormous creative potential and thus a gain for the entire society. Young people, especially, are a tremendous source of creativity, and the more people there are, the more exuberantly is creativity inspired. That viewpoint is absolutely in line with the concept of LaRouche's "relative potential population density."

As the President of the European Chambers of Commerce and Industry, Christoph Leitl, has just correctly stated, as long as Europe itself remains innovative, there is no reason to be afraid of the United States or China. But Europe's creative potential and neo-liberal ideology are incompatible. Support the BüSo, so that the outcome of this issue is positive. If we can not even establish win-win cooperation in Europe, we need not be surprised that China is more attractive to many countries.

zepp-larouche@eir.de

New Deutsche Bank Crisis Puts 2016 LaRouche Plan Back on the Table

by Paul Gallagher.

May 27—The increasingly perilous state of Deutsche Bank, Germany's largest bank—and still likely having the largest exposure to financial derivatives contracts of any bank in the world—has created a stark choice for Germany and Europe. Create the conditions for a dramatic expansion of industrial lending and infrastructure-project credit, in which a Deutsche Bank can flourish if reorganized in the direction its board says it now urgently wants. Or, see the giant bank fail soon, sending shock waves throughout the trans-Atlantic banking systems.

That puts a spotlight back on the proposal to save Deutsche Bank made to the German government in July 2016 by Lyndon LaRouche and Helga Zepp-LaRouche (republished below). And with Chancellor Merkel now visiting Beijing, there is a second spotlight on China's Belt and Road Initiative of great infrastructure projects, which can help create exactly the conditions demanded above, if Germany joins in it.

The current trampling on Italian voters' right to elect a majority government, because that government angers the City of London, Wall Street, and the European Central Bank, is also involved in this banking crisis, as we will see.

'A Very Long Time Dying'

The immediate facts of Deutsche Bank's crisis are being widely reported, but in a manner which obscures their cause, already laid bare in the LaRouche 2016 proposal.

The bank has fired its CEO, John Cryan, a veteran of London's Warburg Bank, the UBS board of directors, and the giant British conglomerate of hedge funds called Man Group. Deutsche Bank Chairman Paul Achleitner survived only by promising to shrink and

cc/Markus Bernet

Deutsche Bank Towers, Frankfurt am Main, Germany.

John Cryan, recently fired Deutsche Bank CEO. He brought to Deutsche Bank the disastrous speculative policies of Warburg Bank, UBS and the giant British conglomerate of hedge funds called the Mann Group.

OO/Gregor Fischer

divest the bank's investment banking divisions, the scene of large losses over recent years. The bank has begun firing between 7,000 and 10,000 of its employees, largely from the investment bank.

An investment analyst from ACG Analytics opined on CNBC May 25 that the bank's stock and capital, recently fallen from 26 billion to 21 billion euros, could soon "go to zero, with very bad consequences for international markets in the near term."

These developments clarify a then-unexplained event of five weeks ago. Germany's *Sueddeutsche Zeitung* (*SDZ*) newspaper for April 16 reported that the European Central Bank (ECB) had told Deutsche Bank to conduct an immediate simulation of what a "crisis scenario" would look like, and what it would cost to carry out a "resolution" of its own investment banking division. The paper said this was the first time the ECB had demanded such a measure from a major bank. "According to the report," *SDZ* wrote, "banking regulators want to know what the impact would be on the value of Deutsche Bank's capital market and derivatives business if … it had to simulate an abrupt end to new business."

Clearly the ECB knew something serious was wrong at the megabank.

A London *Telegraph* columnist jeered on May 24: "it takes a lot to kill off a major bank. They can hang around for a heck of a long time after everyone has forgotten what they were for. And yet, even by the standards of the big beasts of the global finance industry, the once mighty Deutsche Bank has been a very long time dying."

Such *schadenfreude* will take a very short time to turn into panic—including at the ECB—if Deutsche Bank actually fails. It is as leveraged as Lehman was in September 2008. And it is prominent in the City of London-centered phalanx of megabanks which are now choking in highly speculative corporate "junk debt," and derivative contracts on that debt. Now the rise in dollar interest rates is driving them toward mass defaults and the collapse of banks.

Who Ruined Deutsche Bank?

The chief economist of the bank gave an explosive interview to *Handelsblatt* May 23, in which he stated what has ruined it, namely "Anglo-American banking." David Folkerts-Landau described how a team of "star-trader" speculators from Merrill Lynch in London and New York took over Germany's

then-leading bank, starting 20 years ago, and turned it into a giant hedge fund, which made huge profits every year—until it became clear the profits were faked and the bank was all but bankrupt.

Folkerts-Landau placed blame on Josef Ackermann, CEO from 2002 to 2012, among others—not on himself, although he worked within the investment bank throughout those 20 years, and lives in Scotland and the United States. He said Ackermann was seduced by the magic of an annual 25% return on investment apparently produced by the trading floor "stars," who by then had taken over the Deutsche Bank investment bank and were increasingly driving the whole bank with it. Such enormous apparent returns "could only be achieved by accepting major financial and ethical risks," Folkerts-Landau said. He did not explain this, but those risks involved the bank leading the world in exposure to derivatives—complex securities often used to make actual losses appear to be short-term profits. Deutsche Bank played an infamous role in using deceptive derivatives contracts to help bankrupt Monte dei Paschi Bank, Italy's third-largest.

All of this, Folkerts-Landau said, was a "reverse takeover" of the bank by the City of London investment-banking culture of speculation, as opposed to the traditional German banking culture focused on industrial lending and retail commercial banking. "The difficult truth is, fundamental, strategic decisions made by management and the supervisory board from the mid-1990s through 2012, put the bank in this situation.… Since the mid-1990s, the bank's management has left operational and strategic control of its financial markets business to the traders," he told *Handelsblatt*.

The chief economist was

describing how the City of London took over Deutsche Bank after then-CEO Alfred Herrhausen's 1989 assassination, and through "a very long time dying," have brought it near bankruptcy.

LaRouche's Proposal

Returning Deutsche Bank to Herrhausen's banking methods was at the center of the LaRouches' 2016 proposal to save the bank through a German government-organized capital increase, combined with a reorganization and reorientation of the bank's business plan, overseen by a committee created for that purpose.

Now, Deutsche Bank's new CEO, Christian Sewing—with the bank since late in Herrhausen's time—is carrying out deep cuts in the investment bank on which the company has staked and lost so much that it is clearly in peril. And he is pledged to bend the stick back to lending in Germany, industrial investment, and wealth management.

But this requires a change in credit, investment, and international cooperation strategy by Germany. Herrhausen was not a local banker; he was planning such industrial investment for development for the government of Helmut Kohl as Eastern Europe was opening up, when he was assassinated. Now industrial loan demand in Germany has been depressed since the 2008 crash; lack of investment in new infrastructure projects goes back further than that.

Helga Zepp-LaRouche showed that what Alfred Herrhausen proposed in 1989, is what can make a Deutsche Bank reorganization succeed now: "He defended, among other things, the cancellation of the unpayable debt of developing countries, as well as the long-term credit financing of well-defined development projects."

Today that means cooperation and joint credit issuance with the Belt and Road Initiative of China, building land-bridges and maritime routes of new infrastructure across Eurasia into Eastern Europe, Southwest Asia and Africa. In that environment, Deutsche Bank can be saved by the actions Lyndon and Helga LaRouche proposed, before it fails explosively.

Not only has the European Union tried to block Eastern European countries from these cooperative infrastructure projects with China's state commercial banks; it has just refused to allow a majority-elected government in Italy.

That elected government "threatened"—from London-centered financial circles' point of view—to violate rules of the European Central Bank and EU: by expanding infrastructure credit outside the EU's fiscal austerity straightjacket; by recapitalizing banks to save savers and bondholders and allow new lending; and by Glass-Steagall separation of investment banking in order to protect only commercial banking and industrial lending.

These "threats" from Italy to the Eurozone's crippling austerity and "bail-in" rules, have a great deal in common with the measures Lyndon LaRouche proposed to save Deutsche Bank. So the issue is the same in both cases: The Eurozone, with its close ties to City of London banking, is steadily impoverishing half the countries in it, and pushing its own big banks toward bankruptcy and deadly "bail-ins."

LaRouche's 2016 proposal to save Deutsche Bank pointed toward a broader solution to the crisis, and that is now on the table, both in the new crisis of Deutsche Bank, and in the likely upcoming new general election in Italy.

Zepp-LaRouche: Deutsche Bank Must Be Rescued, for the Sake of World Peace!

Helga Zepp-LaRouche, chairwoman of the German Civil Rights Movement Solidarity party, issued the following statement July 12, 2016:

The imminent threat of the bankruptcy of Deutsche Bank is certainly not the only potential trigger for a new systemic crisis of the trans-Atlantic banking system, which would be orders of magnitude more deadly than the 2008 crisis, but it does offer a unique lever to prevent a collapse into chaos.

Behind the SOS launched by the chief economist of Deutsche Bank, David Folkerts-Landau, for an EU program of 150 billion euros to recapitalize the banks, lurks the danger openly discussed in international financial media, that the entire European banking system is de facto insolvent, and is sitting on a mountain of at least 2 trillion euros of non-performing loans. Deutsche Bank is the international bank which, with a total of 55 trillions of outstanding derivative contracts and a leverage factor of 40:1, even outdoes Lehman Brothers at the time of its collapse, and therefore represents the most dangerous Achilles heel of the system. Half of DB's balance sheet, which has plummeted 48% in the past 12 months and is down to only 8% of its peak value, is made up of level-3 derivatives, i.e., derivatives amounting to circa 800 billion without a market valuation.

It probably came as a surprise to many that Lyndon LaRouche called today for Deutsche Bank to be saved through a one-time increase in its capital base, because of the systemic implications of its threatened bankruptcy. Neither the German government with its GDP of 4 trillion euros, nor the EU with a GDP of 18 trillion, would be able to control the domino effect of a disorderly bankruptcy.

The one-time capital injection, LaRouche explained, is only an emergency measure which needs to be followed by an immediate reorientation of the bank, back to its tradition which prevailed until 1989 under the leadership of Alfred Herrhausen. To actually oversee such an operation, a management committee must be set up to verify the legitimacy and the implications of the obligations, and finalize its work within a given timeframe. That committee should also draw up a new business plan, based on Herrhausen's banking philosophy and exclusively oriented to the interests of the real economy of Germany.

Alfred Herrhausen was the last actually creative, moral industrial banker of Germany. He defended, among other things, the cancellation of the unpayable debt of developing countries, as well as the long-term credit financing of well-defined development projects. In December 1989, he planned to present in New York a plan for the industrialization of Poland, which was consistent with the criteria used by the Kreditanstalt fuer Wiederaufbau (KfW) for the post-1945 reconstruction of Germany, and would have offered a completely different perspective than the so-called "reform policy," or shock therapy, of Jeffrey Sachs.

Herrhausen was assassinated on November 30, 1989, by the "Third Generation of the Red Army Fraction," whose existence has yet to be proven to this day. It happened only two days after Chancellor Helmut Kohl, who counted Herrhausen among his closest advisors,

Alfred Herrhausen, assassinated Deutsche Bank chairman.

had presented his ten-point program for gradually overcoming the division of Germany [between East and West]. The *cui bono* of the terrorist attack remains one of the most fateful issues in the modern history of Germany, and one which urgently needs to be clarified.

The fact is that Herrhausen's successors introduced a fundamental paradigm change in the bank's philosophy, which brought Deutsche Bank into the wild world of profit maximization at all costs, and also into countless unpunishable and punishable legal entanglements, which those responsible have avoided until now, mainly because of the "too big to fail" premises.

The transformation of Deutsche Bank into a global investment bank with the highest derivatives exposure, combined with the simultaneous credit crunch for German small and medium-sized enterprises, is symptomatic of the folly which has led to the current catastrophe.

We must now act with resolution, but not in the way Folkerts-Landau proposes; that is, not with more of the same medicine, which would certainly kill the patient. Although it has mainly operated over the past years out of London and New York, Deutsche Bank is too important for the German economy, and therefore for Germany, and ultimately for the fate of all of Europe. Its reorganization in the spirit of Alfred Herrhausen is not only the key to overcoming the banking crisis, but also for averting the acute danger of war.

Herrhausen's assassination has gone unpunished. However, there exists "the dreaded might, that judges what is hid from sight," which is the subject of Friedrich Schiller's poem "Die Kraniche des Ibykus" ["The Cranes of Ibykus"]. The Erinyes have begun their dreadful dance.

It is now incumbent upon all those who, in addition to the family, have suffered from the assassination of Herrhausen, upon the representatives of the Mittelstand, of the German economy and the institutional representatives of the German population, to honor his legacy and to seize the tremendous opportunity which is now offered to save Germany.

China-Singapore Route To Provide Faster Links to Europe for Southeast Asia

by William Jones

May 26—More nations have agreed to join the China-Singapore Connectivity Initiative (CCI) Southern Transport Corridor, an intermodal transport system connecting Chongqing, China, with Singapore, which offers a shorter and more direct trading route between western China and Southeast Asia than that provided by the present route along the Yangtze River to Shanghai.

Chinese provinces such as Sichuan, Henan, and Hunan, as well as countries such as Poland and the United Arab Emirates (UAE), all expressed their wish to help build the corridor at the 10th Pan-Beibu Gulf Economic Cooperation Forum and Second China-Indochina Peninsula Economic Corridor Development Forum, held in southern China's Guangxi Zhuang Autonomous Region on May 24.

The new rail corridor runs from Chongqing in southwest China to the Qinzhou port in Guangxi Province on the Gulf of Tonkin. From there, goods will be carried by ship to Singapore, and will then proceed further along the Maritime Silk Road route to Southeast and Southwest Asia, and further on to the Mediterranean and Europe.

The Southern Transportation Corridor will cut transportation time from the three weeks now needed to ferry goods from Chongqing via river to Shanghai and onward to Singapore by sea, to one week. The new corridor was decided upon in 2017, and has involved close cooperation between Chongqing and Singapore in the areas of financial services, aviation, transport and logistics, and information and communication technology.

In August 2017, Pacific International Lines, along with PSA International and IBM Singapore, signed an MOU to create a Blockchain, a secure, immutable and tamper-resistant ledger that can be used to track shipments. This digital infrastructure can connect parties in the supply chain, giving them access to information and real-time visibility based on their level of permission.

According to the World Economic Forum, by reducing barriers within the international supply chain, global trade could increase by nearly 15 percent.

The construction of the Southern Transport Corridor has made substantial progress since it was launched in 2017. Wei Ran, an official of Guangxi, said that cargo is now transported through the trade route to 58 ports of 35 countries. The corridor has reduced the distance for freight by 1,000 kilometers, and reduced the average travel time of cargo by 12 days. Wei also noted that 660 sea-railway trains, 100 freight trains, and 500 cross-border highway transport vehicles will operate through the route this year, which is believed to bring huge market potential.

The initiative has also encouraged western provinces such as Guangxi, Guizhou, and Gansu to move their goods via railway to the Guangxi port, and from there to Singapore and ports abroad. The CCI-Southern Transport Corridor has been referred to by China's President Xi Jinping as the international land and sea corridor that connects the overland Silk Road Economic Belt with the 21st Century Maritime Silk Road.

November 23, 1998

When Economics Becomes Science

by Lyndon H. LaRouche, Jr.

If a follower of Immanuel Kant could understand it, it can not be true.

Take another look at the two remaining choices which the developments of the past fourteen months now present to the world of 1999. First: What are those foolish ideas, in which the governments and most of the populations of the U.S.A. and western Europe continued to believe during 1998, which now threaten the doom of civilization during the course of 1999? Second: What must be changed, very soon, if civilization is to reach the year 2000 safely? We shall address these questions from the vantage-point of the present state of economic science.

The present situation is, in summary, as follows. Focus upon that situation as it has developed since Spring and Summer 1997.

During more than thirty years, by Spring 1997, I had accumulated a public record in long-range forecasting whose accuracy is unmatched by any other noted economist reporting during that same period.[1] During Summer 1997, I forecast a new turn, as about to erupt.[2] I situated this within the framework defined by what had been published, in 1994, under the title of my "Ninth Forecast." My Summer 1997 update of that "Ninth Forecast," warned, that middle to late October 1997 would see the outbreak of a new, terminal phase,

in the already ongoing, global, systemic financial crisis. I stressed that the present world financial system would never emerge intact from the series of crises which would begin erupting during October 1997. During late October 1997, that new phase erupted in timely fashion.[3]

In the meantime, while western Europe and the U.S.A. hang over the precipice, watching for the doom which threatens to strike during early 1999, the recent months have brought forth a directly contrary, hopeful development, involving forms of cooperation among China and other nations, which could mean that the greatest period in the economic history of our planet would be the dominant feature of the coming century. If the U.S. and some other governments could come to their senses, in time, a way out of the presently ongoing global economic catastrophe is available to us all.

Consider the danger first, and then consider the hopeful alternative.

Unfortunately, during early October 1998, even after twelve months' consistent proof of my forecast, the G-7 governments had foolishly rejected my warnings. These supposedly leading nations of North America, western Europe, and Japan, had chosen exactly

---

1. Lyndon LaRouche, "The Coming Disintegration of Financial Markets," *Executive Intelligence Review*, June 24, 1994.

2. For example, Lyndon H. LaRouche, Jr., interview to "EIR Talks," June 17, 1997, quoted in *Executive Intelligence Review*, June 5, 1986, p. 9.

———, "Your Time Is Running Out," *Executive Intelligence Review*, June 13, 1997.

3. Among the catastrophic events of Black October 1997: Southeast Asia underwent record declines in stocks, assets, and currencies. The Hong Kong stock market lost nearly one-quarter of its value in four days, under speculative attack. On Oct. 27, the Dow Jones Industrial Average dropped 550 points, then rebounded 357 the next day, after the Federal Reserve, IBM, and mutual funds infused massive amounts of funds into key stocks. On Oct. 27-30, there was $10 billion in capital flight from Brazil, and the São Paulo stock market lost 35% of its value. The prime rate was hiked to 43%, slowing the outflow of capital, but further collapsing the domestic economy.

Clockwise from right: Immanuel Kant, Hannah Arendt, Adolf Hitler. "All of my own discoveries in economic science, and in related work," LaRouche writes, "depended upon my earlier commitment to refuting and rejecting that satanic principle of evil which Arendt rightly identifies, and embraces, as embedded, axiomatically, within the work of Kant. It is from that vantage-point, that the general failure of nearly all of the present century's generally accepted academic economists, is best understood." Arendt became a follower of Kant, whom she recognized as a philosophical forerunner of Hitler and the existentialists.

what I had forewarned them against doing. They had launched a hyper-inflationary pump-priming operation, a parody of the hyper-inflationary spiral which Weimar Germany had unleashed upon itself during the years 1921-1923.[4]

Since this past October, until the day this is written, those governments, central bankers, and most of the mass media of those nations, have been obsessed by their professed delusion, that their hyper-inflationary bubble-pumping, led by U.S. Federal Reserve Chairman Alan Greenspan and other doomed ducks of central banking, had brought to an end the financial crises experienced over the year from mid-October 1997 through September 1998.

Meanwhile, the series of successively worsening crises, which I forecast during Summer 1997, continues. The most ominous development of the past thirteen months, as now we approach the end of 1998, has been

a global collapse, since October 1997, in levels of trade and production, with collapses in key sub-sectors of international trade, collapses which range between 20% and 40% in crucial categories. So, just as my Triple

In this Feature

---

4. Lyndon H. LaRouche, Jr., "The Roots of Today's Mass Hysteria," **Executive Intelligence Review**, Nov. 6, 1998; Lyndon H. LaRouche, Jr. "What Each Among All Nations Must Do Now," **Executive Intelligence Review**, Oct. 9, 1998; Richard Freeman, "Greenspan Creates New Hyperinflation Danger," **Executive Intelligence Review**, Nov. 13, 1998; Richard Freeman, "Hyperinflation in Weimar Germany," **Executive Intelligence Review**, Jan. 30, 1998.

A Typical Collapse Function

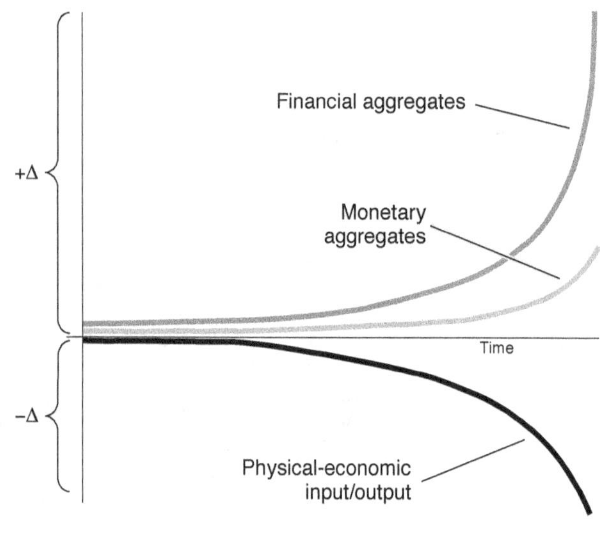

Financial Paper Zooms while Real Economy Collapses

(percent change)

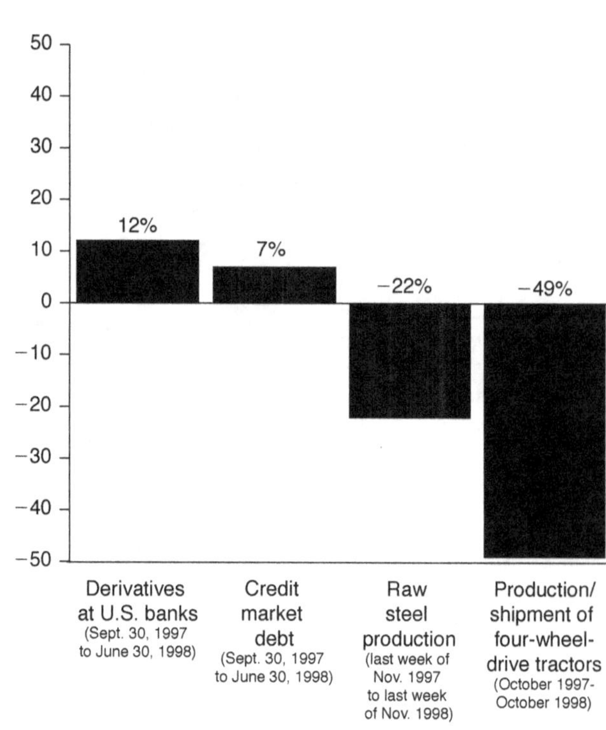

Curve [**Figure 1**] from late 1995 depicts the situation still today, during the interval October 1997 into October 1998 [**Figure 2**], financial hyperinflation of the more wildly speculative categories of financial paper zoomed upward, while production and trade plummeted. The difference between the closing weeks of 1995, when I introduced that curve, and now, is that the fatal boundary-layer depicted in that figure, has now been reached.

The central bankers' latest bookkeeping swindle, the attempt to hide the trade-collapse figures for no more than a couple of months,[5] at most, marks the end of the line—the time when, as the giggling kindergarten children once said it, "all fall down, go boom!"

Some relatively few weeks ahead, Federal Reserve Chairman Alan Greenspan's Weimar-hyperinflation style, financial bubble, will burst. Unless the President of the U.S.A., by then, accepts my guidance in dealing with this crisis, the existing nations of western Europe, and the U.S.A., will be plunged suddenly into the worst existential crisis since no less than the past six centuries of modern European history. Then, not much later than some weeks into 1999, today's orgy of desperate delusions will come to an end, buried under history's greatest trashing of paper fool's gold.

The U.S.A. and western Europe will then be plunged into something awesomely worse than the worst economic depression in six centuries. Unless the measures which I have proposed, are implemented soon, most of those nations, including Bill Clinton's U.S.A., will begin to disintegrate as nations, as an early result of that collapse.[6]

This catastrophe, *if it were not prevented*, would not be something some imaginary Gods of Olympus have done to us. Such an apocalyptic catastrophe would be what the foolish majority of the American people, among others, had done to themselves. Such is the price popular opinion would have paid for flights from reality, into silly dreams, into its own wishful, delusory views on matters of economics and politics.

Today, the most numerous, very silliest among government officials and central bankers of the U.S.A. and western Europe, **insist** on continuing the policy which

---

5. There are efforts to juggle the trade and payments accounts among a number of nations, to the purpose of concealing, for at least one or two months, the disastrous collapse of the balance of trade levels of a number of states, including the U.S.A.

6. Lyndon H. LaRouche, Jr., "Is Western Europe Doomed?" *Executive Intelligence Review*, Nov. 27, 1998.

has caused this calamity. They insist, foolishly, stubbornly, that the system of "free trade" and "globalization" must triumph, unchallenged, during the weeks to come. If that foolish public opinion prevails, then we can surely say, that those governments, those central banking systems, and also the ordinary inhabitants of those nations, have doomed themselves to join the ranks of all ancient empires which have fallen into the dust of time.

So, if such folk continue to cling to their presently expressed beliefs, doom is the experience which today's mayfly dreamers, and others, will come soon to enjoy, beginning some time during the course of the weeks ahead.

So, I repeat the warning made earlier. It is today's popular superstitions about economics, superstitions such as "post-industrial" utopianism, "free trade," and "globalization," which are at the root of the ongoing catastrophe. We must emphasize once more: These silly, popular superstitions, which have been embedded as fads, during the recent three decades' policy-shaping of the G-7 monetary authorities, are the continuing cause for the impending disintegration of what is often called "Western civilization" today. Unless those faddish policies are suddenly, effectively reversed, during the weeks immediately ahead, "Western civilization," and you, my friend, with it, are already doomed to plunge into a process of disintegration, beginning early during the course of 1999.

Latin, For Example

As I have stressed in earlier reports on this subject, the root-causes of this looming doom, were established as potential, as a potentially fatal susceptibility, long before the Twentieth Century. What has changed lately, is that that potential doom has become, increasingly, a virtually certain one. What changed, about thirty-odd years ago, is that what had been formerly no worse than a lurking potential catastrophe, became the accelerating onrush of an actual apocalypse. So it was, centuries and millennia earlier, with all the once-powerful, fallen empires which lie now in the dust of past ages. The ordinary people, as well as the political leaders of those doomed empires of the past, each in his or her own fashion, contributed to bringing doom upon themselves.

Usually, the people of those self-doomed former empires, especially the leaders, refused to recognize their doom even when it was already looking them directly in the eye. For us, as it was for them, despite the outward grandeur of what contemporaries saw as unshakable, almost eternal power, there is a potentially fatal folly slinking, menacingly, among the shadows, while the fools are distracted by the customary parade of colorful, day-to-day, stock-market and other popular delusions, passing pompously in review.

For example, about a decade ago, in just such a fashion, just weeks before the disintegration of the Berlin Wall, the already doomed dictator of the German Democratic Republic, Erich Honecker, and his prize-winning admirer, Canada's Edgar Bronfman, proudly asserted the almost everlasting durability of that already doomed nation.[7] In such a fashion, silly geese of Europe, as of North America, speak desperately, hysterically of a recovery now in progress, when doom is clearly visible on the way.

So, even the most powerful nations may be doomed by the persistence, over successive generations, of what later appears as those traditions, those inclinations, by means of which they brought doom upon themselves. Thus, we must say, that those persons, in the U.S.A. and western Europe, who do not master the relevant lessons of past history, are persons who have lacked the most essential of those elements of knowledge indispensable to people who command the moral fitness to survive these times of troubles immediately ahead. Such are the considerations upon which the continued existence of the economies of nations such as the U.S.A., depend absolutely today.

I concede, that even at this late date, it might still be useful to have learned ancient Latin, if only so that you might understand that doomed culture of ancient Rome

____

7. Edgar Bronfman met with East German dictator Erich Honecker on Oct. 17, 1988, during which he was awarded the East German medal of the "Peoples Friendship in Gold." On Nov. 30, 1989, World Jewish Congress representative Maram Stern assured East Germany's Foreign Minister of the WJC's opposition to reunification, and saying that WJC "President Bronfman would exert his influence in this direction in the U.S. and elsewhere." He continued, "In any case, the WJC will do everything possible to strengthen the G.D.R. [East Germany] politically and economically." In 1989, Honecker had proclaimed for the 40th anniversary of the German Democratic Republic, *"Den Sozialismus in seinem Lauf hält weder Ochs noch Esel auf"* ("Socialism in its course, can be stopped by neither ox nor ass"). Notwithstanding, he was ousted as communist party head on Oct. 18, 1989, and after a brief interregnum, was replaced by Hans Modrow, who was voted out in March 1990.

Praxiteles' sculpture of "Hermes with the Infant Dionysius" (one of the few surviving Greek sculptures, as opposed to Roman-era reproductions), clearly shows the superiority of Greek civilization over the stultified Roman culture, as shown by this drawing of the Roman "Apollo of the Belvedere."

better, as St. Augustine did, and might, therefore, be less likely to repeat the follies of that Latin empire, as most of your fellow-citizens have been doing lately.[8] Better than learning Latin, it is more useful to learn Plato's Classical Greek.

On precisely this account, I have lately stressed, repeatedly, that there is an urgent lesson for today, to be learned from a long sweep of history, beginning in Egypt, even centuries before the birth of Christ. An adequate understanding of the combined ancient, medieval, and modern history of European civilization, depends upon an understanding of why Roman civilization was doomed from the outset.

This point is most simply and clearly illustrated by attention to recently rediscovered evidence bearing upon a most crucial single, included fact. That fact, as I addressed it, yet once more, in an address I delivered at Bad Schwalbach, Germany, this past November 22,[9] is,

that more than 1,723 years elapsed, between that discovery of South America which was claimed for Egypt, on August 5, 231 B.C., and the claim of the discovery of the Americas, for Spain, dated as October 12, 1492. The crucial fact is, that the voyage of Christopher Columbus was based upon rediscovery, during the mid-Fifteenth Century, of the same scientific principles which had guided Egypt's trans-Pacific 233-231 B.C. voyage of discovery, 1,723 years earlier.

Admittedly, there are indications of other voyages to the Americas, from across the Pacific, before the Egyptian discovery of 231 B.C.; there were certainly earlier voyages, from the Straits of Gibraltar across the Atlantic, before Columbus. The distinction of the Egyptian discovery of South America from chance voyages which did occur, or may have occurred, was that it was a voyage based then on an explicitly specified scientific certainty, not chance impulses; Columbus' voyage, too, was based upon rediscovery of that same scientific certainty, not accidents, guesses, or chance.

The crucial fact within that historical connection be-

---

8. St. Augustine, **Concerning the City of God against the Pagans**, Henry Bettenson, trans. (New York: Penguin Books, 1972).

9. Conference on "History As a Principle of Action," speech by LaRouche on "What Is Real History, As Science? All Modern Science Is Based on Erathosthenes' Work on Determining the Shape of the Earth." See also LaRouche et al., "Go With the Flow: Why Scholars Lied About Ulysses' Transatlantic Crossing," **Executive Intelligence Review**, Nov.

20, 1998. Reports on this subject will also be published in the Winter 1998-1999 edition of **21st Century Science & Technology**, and subsequent issues.

tween the discoveries of 231 B.C. and A.D. 1492, is, once more, that both voyages of discovery were based upon the same principles of science, the principles discovered and developed by the great continuer of the scientific method of Plato's Academy, Eratosthenes, the principles copied by the associates of Cardinal Nicholas of Cusa, during the middle of the Fifteenth Century.[10] Thus, the 1,723 years between those two voyages, represent the duration of a period of loss of scientific knowledge, a long dark age which descended upon the Mediterranean region, with the rise of the Latin-speaking Romans to power. It was those relatively brutish Latin speakers, who prevailed over the culturally superior Greeks of the preceding two centuries of Classical and Hellenistic times, who dragged most of European civilization to doom with them.

The crucial point should be restated: that nearly fifteen centuries elapsed between the birth of Christ and his apostles, and the qualified triumph of Christian principles of statecraft, after a long struggle, led by Christians following in the footsteps of Peter, John, Paul, and their follower Augustinus, against the ruinous legacy of the "New Babylon," Rome and its empire.[11] The ironical murder of Eratosthenes' collaborator, Archimedes, by Roman soldiers, most aptly typifies the evil—the cultural and moral depravity—which the "New Babylon," ancient Rome, like Babylon and Tyre before it, represented throughout the Mediterranean region.

The same, corrosive influence, which was responsible for that 1,723-year interval in the lapse of science, is echoed, once again, in the history of statecraft in Europe itself, during the approximately five centuries since Columbus' voyages of discovery and exploration. In both cases, ancient and modern alike, the nature of the relevant evidence is the same: a looming catastrophe caused by nothing other than the willful suppression of certain scientific principles which were essential for the progress of civilization.

In the first instance, during the 1,723-year interval prior to the collaboration of Cusa with his friend Toscanelli, what was lost from practice, was the driving principle and method of the development of Classical Greek science, from Thales and Pythagoras through the Platonic Academy of Plato through Eratosthenes.

In the second instance, following Venice's defeat of the League of Cambrai, what was lost, in large degree, was that method of Plato's Academy, the science which had been revived under Nicholas of Cusa and his successors. This revived science was, tragically, replaced by the Latin-like neo-Aristoteleanism of Venice's Padua,[12] and, even worse, that empiricist method of Venice's Paolo Sarpi. It is from Sarpi's empiricism that the presently ruinous, gnostic dogmas of "free trade" and "globalization" are derived.

The legacy of Babylon, which ancient Rome bequeathed to feudal Europe, is echoed in the roles which Venice and, later, today's British monarchy, have represented, in succession, for more than 1,000 years until now.

Since the beginning of the Sixteenth Century, since the defeat of the League of Cambrai by Venice and its Spanish allies, the leading landed aristocracies and financial oligarchies of Europe have been engaged in a desperate effort to turn back the clock, to a feudalistic, post-nation-state globalization, a desperate effort to crush and eliminate the institutions of the modern nation-state and those other institutions which are best typified today by the 1776 Declaration of Independence and 1789 Federal Constitution of the U.S.A.

Since A.D. 1510-1511, that reactionary effort to turn back the clock, was never entirely defeated, but, until events erupting in the aftermath of the 1962 Cuba Missiles Crisis,[13] never actually succeeded, either.

The aftermath of that 1962 crisis, included such notable events as the October 15, 1963 retirement of Chancellor Konrad Adenauer in Germany, the attempted assassinations of President Charles de Gaulle, the November 22, 1963 assassination of a President Kennedy who was targetted by the same circles behind the attempted assassinations of de Gaulle,[14] the subse-

<hr>

10. "Columbus and the Christian Conception of Man," *Fidelio*, Spring 1992, and *Ibykus* No. 38, 1992.

11. See St. John on "The Whore of Babylon," *Apocalypse*. Pagan Rome of the Caesars was, in fact, a revival of the tradition of the empires of ancient Mesopotamia, empires consistent with what had been known earlier as the "Persian," or "oligarchical" model. Hence, to identify the principle of Roman rule as "The Whore of Babylon," is literally true.

12. e.g., the "mortalist" Pietro Pomponazzi and his student Cardinal Gasparo Contarini.

13. Lyndon H. LaRouche, Jr., et al., "How Our World Was Nearly Destroyed," *Strategic Studies*, **Executive Intelligence Review**, Oct. 23, 1998.

———, "Is Western Europe Doomed?" **Executive Intelligence Review**, Nov. 27, 1998.

14. Despite the hysterical efforts of John J. McCloy, et al., to force the Warren Commission into adopting the infamous cover-up of the Kennedy assassination, the agencies known to have targetted President Kennedy for assassination (whoever actually conducted the attack) were the same British intelligence circles identified by French authori-

quent November 30, 1966 cold coup d'état against Adenauer's successor, Ludwig Erhard, and the subsequent, April 28, 1969, ouster of de Gaulle. These developments correspond to a fundamental change in axioms of policy-making, which was imposed upon both the U.S.A. and continental western Europe in the wake of the 1962 Cuba Missiles Crisis. The world of President Franklin Roosevelt, Douglas MacArthur, Adenauer, de Gaulle, Kennedy, and Erhard, was willfully pushed from the stage by the authors of what became known as the "New Age" of "post-industrial utopia, "free trade," and post-nation-state "globalization;" the march of the "New Age's" political lemmings toward the cliffs, had begun.[15]

Thus, following that 1962 crisis, with the spread of the manias of "post-industrial" utopianism, "free trade," and "globalization," we face now the likelihood that the neo-feudalists might finally succeed in setting up their kind of anti-science-motivated "world government," that utopia of the damned called "globalization." They themselves would not survive to enjoy their pyrrhic victory. They, too, would be destroyed by their own victory over the forces of reason; their victory would mean the apocalyptic doom of us all, a plunge of this planet, or at least western European civilization, into the worst dark age since the well-earned doom which a Latin-misruled European civilization suffered earlier, in the disintegration of the Roman Empire.

The comparison of an ancient European culture self-doomed by the influence of Rome, to the threatened doom of European civilization at the present moment, is appropriate in a degree which some might find awesome, once they grasp the essential connections. There is a deep connection, between the corrosive impact of Latin culture upon the Mediterranean region, then, and the influences which have been responsible for the incompetence of nearly all contemporary economists today. I refer to those factors of incompetence, which are responsible for the past thirty-odd years slide toward doom of what had been, in 1962-1963, the world's most powerful, and, then, still-growing economic system.

---

ties as engaged in the targetting of President Charles de Gaulle. The Profumo scandal, used to oust Britain's Prime Minister Harold Macmillan, is part of the same bloc of actions which resulted in the elimination of powerful U.S. and European political leaders opposed to the policies of post-industrial utopia pushed by McCloy and his crowd.
15. ibid.

Science & Economy

As I have just emphasized, above, the essential reason for the doom of a civilization polluted by Latin culture's influence, is typified by the decline of the dominant science-culture of the Mediterranean region, that of Egypt's Hellenistic science, from the level represented by Eratosthenes, to the decadence represented by the anti-heliocentric hoax perpetrated by Claudius Ptolemy, that anti-heliocentric superstition still faithfully defended by corrupted influential circles in Europe as late as the Seventeenth Century.[16]

With the rise of the power of Rome, the principle of scientific truthfulness, upon which Plato's Academy had premised scientific practice, was pushed aside. It was the policy of slavery and looting inhering in Latin thought, which defined Rome as a culture which lacked the moral fitness to survive. Where even plain economic truth conflicted with Latin prejudice, truth was pushed aside, and truth then destroyed the culture which had rejected its own moral fitness to survive.

Today's popular delusion is, that "economics" is "about money," "price," or, "how to succeed in the business world." Such beliefs are not only morally degrading fads; they border upon insanity in their effects. They are the kinds of mass delusions which will cause a nation to destroy itself. In contrast to such delusions, in reality, economics is the subject of the human species' relationship to nature; it is, as Leibniz defined it, primarily a matter of the role which the development of the innate creative powers of the individual mind must play, in increasing mankind's mastery over nature. While that relationship is not limited to what physical science is narrowly defined to be today, the role of scientific and technological progress is a crucial part of economic processes. Those who ignore the determining role of scientific progress, as today's "New Age ecologists" and the Mont Pelerin Society's "free trade" freaks do, bring doom upon themselves, and, if they are successful, all of civilization, too.

There is more than a mere parallel to Rome's self-induced doom, in the influence of the British empiricist hoaxes of Paolo Sarpi's followers. As in the case of Sir Isaac Newton's "action at a distance" hoax, expressed in the guise of "free trade" dogma, empiricism's corrupting, collateral impact upon contemporary eco-

---

16. Robert R. Newton, *The Crime of Claudius Ptolemy* (Baltimore: Johns Hopkins University Press, 1977).

nomic policy, is destroying civilization from within. Just as Rome's toleration for the practice of slavery, defined it, like Jefferson Davis's and Robert E. Lee's Confederacy, as a society whose conception of human nature was so degraded that that nation's political existence must be exterminated: so, both ancient Rome and the modern British monarchy. Just as a society which accepted the culture of Rome, had lost the moral fitness to survive, so, a modern economy which adapted itself to the lunatic, pro-oligarchical methods of "post-industrial" utopia, "free trade," and "globalization," represents a misconception of the nature of man, which the Creator of this universe will not tolerate indefinitely.

Once the U.S.A. and leading nations of continental Europe chose to break altogether with American System tradition, and go the British "free trade" way, in the aftermath of the 1962 Cuba Missiles Crisis, the worm of "New Age" rot within European civilization, took over. The presently ongoing disintegration of that civilization, world wide, is the result of that fatal error of the mid-1960s, the error of choosing to become a power which has abandoned the moral fitness to survive. A rejection of the truth respecting man's relationship to nature, the policy of slavery, was the cause of the collapse of the Roman empire, just as any present continuation of the unnatural policy of unbridled "free trade," assures the collapse of Western civilization today.

Thus, in the aftermath of the Cuba Missiles Crisis, European civilization brought itself, step by step, toward the edge of doom. The legendary "New Age" of the radical Sixty-Eighters, is now surely doomed. Only a precious short time remains, for the President of the U.S.A. to reverse what has been his own administration's social and economic policies until now. Otherwise, the entirety of Western European civilization will disintegrate, not gradually, but in violent convulsions, during the months ahead.

Those background considerations so restated, we come now to the core of the matter to be addressed in this report. Just as the scientific principles represented by the work of Eratosthenes, draw the line between the superior qualities of Hellenistic culture, and the contrasting, anti-scientific characteristics which doomed Rome, so we may point to a specific principle of scientific work which draws the line between the possibility of a recovery of the world's economy, even at this late date, and the inevitable doom of Western civilization, unless that corrective principle of science is adopted now.

On this account, my role in economic science continues to be, historically, a uniquely essential one. What ought to be taken as the astonishing fact about my own achievements in this branch of science, is only the fact that no one else made the same crucial, readily available, presently indispensable set of discoveries. *Any literate and intelligent young person who put his mind to the same task, and pursued it with the degree of impassioned devotion I did, could have made the same discoveries. Why didn't they?* There lies the source of the threat of doom lurking at the flanks of western Europe and the U.S.A. during the crisis-ridden weeks and months ahead.

There was a certain progress in the further development of economic science (as distinct from its useful application), following the 1671-1716 founding of the science of physical economy, by Gottfried Leibniz. Although Leibniz's economic science was spread in the form of what became known as Treasury Secretary Alexander Hamilton's American System of political-economy, the progress in discovery of new principles halted after the contributions of France's Lazare Carnot. The work of the Careys and Friedrich List typify the progress of the American System economists in developing *the application of* the previously discovered scientific principles defined by Leibniz and Lazare Carnot. No fundamental progress in mastering actually new principles of that science was made, after the crucial contributions of Carnot on the machine-tool principle, until my own work of the 1948-1952 interval. Even now, more than forty-five years later, my original contributions, although they are increasingly widely known, remain unique.

How could such long periods of lapse in scientific progress occur?

For an appropriate comparison, think of the parallel to the period of creeping, Latin-speaking darkness of the mind, during the centuries following the deaths of Eratosthenes and Archimedes. Certainly, the physical and other relevant attributes of the minds of Mediterranean populations represented the same biological potentials as members of Plato's Academy such as Eratosthenes. Why no new Eratosthenes? In present-day street-jargon: under the conditions favoring growing Roman influence throughout the region, there was a diminishing market for the work of minds like theirs. Under such conditions of prevailing immorality today, a diminishing ration of students have sufficient devotion to truth for its own sake—Plato's principle of *agapē*, to pursue a career for which no financially rewarding, or popularly prestigious places of employment are advertised. On this account, when it comes to choosing future careers, the name for banality is, thus, often: "Hey, Joe, let's be practical! Pick a career that pays, instead."

Once more, summarize the history of economic science up to the present time.

Economic science was begun by Gottfried Leibniz, beginning approximately 1671-1672, continuing through approximately the time of his death. Leibniz defined it as a science of physical economy, as I do today. Every successful version of economic science practiced thereafter, including the economics on which the U.S. economy was originally premised, and including my own practice, was based upon the work and influence of Leibniz. Economic science consisted of the adaptation of the principles discovered chiefly by Leibniz and Carnot to the benefits of modern physical science in general. After the work of Carnot, no new validated principle of economic science as such was provided, until my own original work done over the 1948-1952 interval. Until then, the only substantial addition to Leibniz's discoveries were, as I have said, those of Lazare Carnot and his associates, in their development of the principles of application of machine-tool design, these the foundations for later development of the American and German models of the successful modern agro-industrial economy.

What I accomplished was centered, essentially, around two issues. The combined use of the example of the principle of machine-tool design, and my refutation of the central proposition of Immanuel Kant's *Critiques*, to show the absurdity of Norbert Wiener's "information theory," and also to refute the central proposition of John von Neumann's doctrine of "systems analysis." This led me to important original discoveries in the field of epistemology, revolutionizing the science of physical economy in this way. The application of my own original discoveries, then depended for their realization, chiefly, upon using the notions of multiply-connected manifolds provided by Gauss's follower Bernhard Riemann.

If one reviews the elementary nature of my own essential discoveries, it would appear, therefore, that a fairly large number of serious young thinkers should have duplicated the same discoveries which I have achieved, *had they wished to do so.* What prevented them? The answer to that question ought to remind literate readers of Poe's "The Case of the Purloined Letter."

Ask: What is filed, openly, exactly in the place you would expect it to be filed, which informs you exactly why my discovery would be rejected out of hand by virtually all candidates for doctoral degrees in physical science fields today? How does that fact, so easily found on open book-shelves of almost every modern public library, tend to ensure why every person seeking a successful career in any field of science, would shun all evidence leading to my discovery, as a threat to their careers and pensions. Look, for example, under "generally accepted classroom mathematics." Look, for example, under "Isaac Newton."

So, as Poe illustrated the point, the most general of important, truthful facts, are usually hidden in such obvious places, that most ordinary seekers might never think to look for important discoveries there.

On Hannah Arendt's Confession

Whether in physical science, or in Classical art, whether as student, original composer, or performer, knowledge is acquired by two steps. The second, is making, and validating a discovery of principle; but, the first, is defining, and needing to destroy, the obstacle which that discovery overcomes. In our universe, which Leibniz defines as the best of all possible worlds, the recognition of the face of the adversary, evil, is often the first step toward the good. On this account, even a creature as passionately evil as Adolf Hitler, or the "Pirate Jenny" from Bertolt Brecht's **Three-Penny Opera**, or that real-life "Pirate Jenny" known as Nazi Martin Heidegger's lover, Hannah Arendt, may provoke some among us to do something good, as I demonstrate such a connection here and now.

Had the satanic, existentialist pair of Theodor Adorno and Hannah Arendt, not been, quite accidentally, of Jewish ancestry, they would have qualified for, and would probably have become Nazi Party ideologues, like their anti-Semitic crony, Nazi philosopher Martin Heidegger.[17] Hannah was a witch, and a very

---

17. Heidegger obtained a teaching post at Freiburg University, and became a leader of the Nazi student movement, from which position he had his professor, the phenomenologist Edmund Hüsserl, kicked out of the school.

As for Adorno, after the Nazis came to power, he attempted to get a job as music critic with the liberal **Voss'sche Zeitung**. Adorno's article

nasty one, too, the kind of perverse creature who, one could believe, would have found the satanic Heidegger sexually attractive; but, she was also a smart witch, if never an honest one, as the devil's disciples sometimes are.

Arendt's only discernible service to humanity is provoked by the hideous shamelessness of her typically existentialist perversity, the shamelessness with which she became an avowed follower of my legendary adversary, Immanuel Kant. An associate recently led my attention to an exceptionally relevant instance, first published in a 1946 edition of the periodical ***Partisan Review***, where she, in her own perverse fashion, damned that proto-Nazi philosopher, Immanuel Kant, by praising him. She recognized Kant, quite accurately, as a true, if distant progenitor of the kind of irrationalist sophistries upon which Nazi ideological types such as Karl Jaspers, Martin Heidegger, and Jean-Paul Sartre had built the Twentieth-Century existentialism of the followers of Friedrich Nietzsche and Richard Wagner. Ironically, Arendt's praise of Kant as a proto-Nazi, was written in 1946, after she, born a Jew, had witnessed the Nazi experience, and the role of her former lover, Heidegger, as a leading Nazi philosopher, and his role as a persecutor of Jews at Freiburg University.[18]

Like her accomplice Adorno, she, apparently, never actually became formally a Nazi, and certainly did become a prominent anti-Nazi, in her own fashion. Yet, it would be a grave moral, as well as merely factual error, to object to our reporting the plain fact, that all her adult life, even after the Nazi experience, she represented, like her lover Heidegger, like Theodor Adorno, and the Jaspers she also admired, a variety of ideology which was of the same general existentialist species as Hitler's. Referring to the well-known kinships among Jaspers, Heidegger, and Martin Buber, should help to refresh our recollection on such connections. All of these varieties are just as evil, just as dangerous, or, given a chance, even more so, than Hitler's variety, although differing slightly among themselves on secondary, collateral features.[19] Arendt's emphasis on her claimed debt to Kant, points directly toward the relevant point on this account.

Many relevant things could be said truthfully of Arendt and her sort. For our purposes here, it is sufficient to stress the point, that if you understand Hannah Arendt's professed devotion to Kant, you understand what is rotten in the economics and philosophy departments of most of the universities of European civilization today. In a time when foolish academics, and others, still praise Kant, or consider him no worse than a harmless fool, Arendt performed the exemplary, if perverse service of emphasizing what an evil, and dangerous creature Kant was, and still is, today. With one important qualification, which I supply below, there was not only some historical fallacy of composition,

---

(which appeared in ***Die Musik***, Vol. 1934, p. 712 f) heaped praise on a composition by Herbert Münzel, "Die Fahnen der Verfolgten," a musical setting for the poems of Hitler Youth leader Baldur von Schirach. Adorno said of Münzel's work that, "by choosing the poems of von Schirach, it is consciously marked as National Socialist." Adorno was not hired, but only because the Nazis shut down the publication. See, Rolf Wiggershaus, ***Die Frankfurter Schule*** (Munich: DTV, 1988, pp. 178-80.)

18. The following quotation from Arendt appeared in "What Is Existenz Philosophy?," ***Partisan Review***, 1946, under the subhead "Kant's demolition of the Old World and Schelling's cry for a new one": 'The unity of Being and thought presupposed the pre-established coincidence of essence and existence, that, namely, everything thinkable also exists and every existent, because it is knowable, must also be rational. This unity was destroyed by Kant, the true, if also clandestine, founder of the new philosophy: who has likewise remained till the present time its secret king. Kant's proof of the antinomy-structure of Reason, and his analysis of synthetic propositions which proves that in every proposition in which something is asserted about Reality we go beyond the concept (the *essentia*) of a given thing—had already robbed man of the ancient security in Being. Even Christianity had not attacked this security, but only reinterpreted it within "God's plan of salvation."

Arendt proceeds to show the development, out of this, of Existenz philosophy, whose true "modern" founder, Karl Jaspers, she assesses in the final section. To him she also attributes the conceptual groundwork that would later constitute the kernel of her own definition of "authoritarian" and "totalitarian":

"Jaspers holds that in philosophy every ontology claiming it can say what Being really is, in a Slipping-away into the absolutizing of particular categories of Being. The existential meaning of such Slipping-away would be that such a philosophy robs Man of a freedom which can persist only as long as Man does not know what Being really is."

19. Had Germany not lost two world wars, it would be the British monarchy, rather than the Nazi regime, which would have gone down in today's popular opinion as typical of the most evil agencies of the past two or more centuries of world history. Certainly, as measured in death-tolls, and nakedly malicious monstrosities, the crimes for which the British monarchy might be put into a Nuremberg-style dock, outnumber in savagery and scope, even the crimes of the Hitler regime. Certainly, what the Duke of Edinburgh and his crony, and Nazi SS veteran Prince Bernhard, have done in promoting genocide against Africans and others, exceeds the magnitude of the Nuremberg crimes totalled by the Nazi regime. Popular expressions of righteous indignation are usually to be recognized by actually honest and intelligent people as expressing the most outrageous extremes of hypocrisy, and, often, even outright lying.

but also a kernel of truth in her claimed connection to Kant.

As Arendt stresses the crucial fact, with the writing and publication of his *Critiques*, former David Hume devotee Immanuel Kant devoted the concluding decades of his wretched life to denying the existence of both reason and morals (*Vernunft*). The fact that Kant had rejected certain aspects of Hume's argument, to argue the same essential conclusions of Hume from a scholastic, rather than a strictly empiricist standpoint, has fooled many careless academics, but not Heinrich Heine, into mistaking Kant for a rational person.

The simple, if awkwardly argued denial of reason, constitutes the entirety of Kant's **Critique of Pure Reason**. In his later **Critique of Practical Reason**, notably in the section devoted to "The Dialectic of Practical Reason," he anticipates Dr. Sigmund Freud in denying any form of morality but "negation of the negation." In the last of his series of *Critiques*, **The Critique of Judgment**, he lays the foundations for an axiomatically irrationalist, Romantic doctrine of *Volksgeist*, which provides the foundation for the post-1815 teachings of the two cronies G.W.F. Hegel and Karl Savigny, those two ranking among the cornerstones upon which the later development of Nazi ideology was founded.

Heinrich Heine was right to smell the embryo of something like Adolf Hitler, gestating in Kant's womb. Knowing Heine, we must be certain that he would have recognized the evil in Arendt, as he had seen the same evil in Jacques Necker's daughter, the notorious Madame de Staël.[20]

If we were to overlook those relevant points which she evades discussing, she appears to argue a case, this with telling and well-focussed precision, that Kant's denial of the existence of truth and reason, laid the foundations for what was, in fact, the rise of the kind of pro-Nazi existentialism typified by the influence of Jaspers and Heidegger in Hitler Germany, and also Heidegger's rubbish-bin Voltaire, Jean-Paul Sartre. On this point, Arendt professed her admiration for Kant; on that narrower point of her scholarship, the witch was apparently right. It was the issues she carefully evaded by her fallacy of historical composition, which make her own case more interesting for us here.

---

20. On Madame de Staël and Romanticism, see, for example, Heine's *On the History of Religion and Philosophy in Germany*, in **Works of Prose, by Heinrich Heine**, Hermann Kester, ed., Ernst Basch, trans. (New York: L.B. Fischer, 1943).

Science Versus Satan

All of my own discoveries in economic science, and in related work, depended upon my earlier commitment to refuting and rejecting that satanic principle of evil which Arendt rightly identifies, and embraces, as embedded, axiomatically, within the work of Kant. It is from that vantage-point, that the general failure of nearly all of the present century's generally accepted academic economists, is best understood. To set the corner-stone for constructing this report, we shall now compare and contrast the standpoints of Arendt and Kant, and, on that basis, contrast the false opinion of today's so-called leading economists and economic policy-shapers, to the most fundamental principles of modern science and Classical art. In this fashion, we shall expose the reasons why progress in economics as a science, halted after the work of Leibniz and Carnot, until my own discoveries of now nearly a half-century ago.

According to the accounts given by Luca Pacioli, Leonardo da Vinci, and Johannes Kepler, modern experimental European science takes its origin from works on scientific method by Cardinal Nicholas of Cusa, beginning his *De docta ignorantia*. Those accounts are corroborated by examination of the content of the work of these discoverers. Leibniz's work, most notably, was premised on the work of these predecessors; this is most remarkable in the matter of Leibniz's original discovery of a working form of the calculus, a calculus, based upon non-linearity in the infinitesimally small, which Leibniz derived from the specifications given by Kepler.

The root of this method, from Cusa through Leibniz, from Leonardo da Vinci through J.S. Bach, and beyond, is the method of Plato. This Leibniz emphasized in writing two Socratic dialogues, which he dedicated to the purpose of showing the application of Plato's method to the epistemological issues of scientific discovery.[21] While some persons who were otherwise known as advocates of the relatively sterile intellectual methods of Aristoteleanism and empiricism, have made marginal, even original contributions of some importance, the foundations of all modern scientific achieve-

---

21. Gottfried Leibniz, "Dialog über die Verknüpfung zwischen Dingen und Worten," **Leibniz: Hauptschriften zür Grundlegung der Philosophie**, Vol. I (Hamburg: Felix Meiner Verlag, 1966), and *Confessio Philosophi* (Frankfurt: Vittorio Klostermann, 1994).

ment are found in the Platonic method, both as expressed by Classical Greek sources, and by the revival of Plato's method by Cusa, Pacioli, Leonardo, Kepler, Leibniz, et al.

Considering the fact, that all progress in lifting man from out of the bowels of feudalism, depends upon the fruits of the Fifteenth-Century revival of Platonic method, whence such spawn of Hell as an Arendt or the John von Neumann of "systems analysis" notoriety? The answer is supplied, if only implicitly, by Arendt; the difference between my point of view, on the one side, and that of Arendt, Hitler, George Soros, John Locke, and Heidegger's Jean-Paul Sartre, on the other, is a fundamental, unbridgeable difference respecting the definition of individual human nature.[22]

This difference in the conception of human nature, is the same difference, the principle of truth and justice (*agapē*), which Plato elaborates in Book II of his ***The Republic***, as the differences among the dialogue's principal characters there: Socrates, Thrasymachus, and Glaucon. The issue between Socrates and Thrasymachus, is the same difference which Professor Friedrich Freiherr von der Heydte stresses, in his ***Die Geburtsstunde des souveränen Staates***,[23] as the distinction between modern nation-state law, and, on the opposing side, the Thrasymachus-like principles of pre-nation-state, feudal-imperial law, the exact imitation of Thrasymachus taught by the evil John Locke, and practiced by our present-day, degenerated U.S. Department of Justice.

In contrast to the natural law defined by ***The Republic***'s Socrates, the standpoint of Thrasymachus is explicitly the irrationalist kernel of that Romantic notion of law of Prussian state philosopher G.W.F. Hegel's defense of Prince Metternich's Carlsbad *Beschlüsse* [Decrees], and by the neo-Kantian Romantic school of law of Hegel's crony K. Savigny. The same rejection of the

principle of truth is the central axiomatic feature of all of Kant's *Critiques*, a rejection of truthfulness which is asserted with utter shamelessness, in Kant's ***Critique of Judgment***. That far, Arendt's praise of the kernel of irrationalism pervading Kant's *Critiques*, is soundly rooted in her defense of the tyrannical irrationalism of Thrasymachus—the tyranny of arbitrary opinion, against reason—which is characteristic of all modern neo-feudalists, the Romantics Kant, Hegel, Savigny included, and the present-day advocates of the form of neo-feudalism called "globalization" included. For her, truth is the enemy; truth is, for her, "authoritarian." Hers is therefore a suitable doctrine for adoption by a witch in service to the father of lies.

We shall turn to the matter of human nature shortly. First, we must clear up an otherwise confusing, and distracting, point of difference between Kant and overtly satanic Arendt; if only on this one point, she resorts to a fallacy of historical composition, to misrepresent her debt to Kant as a more or less simple, academic sort of connection.

Kant's proposal for "perpetual peace," is to be recognized as a forerunner of Bertrand Russell's, High Commissioner John J. McCloy's, and the Duke of Edinburgh's notions of "transparency," "world religion," and "globalization": of "peace through world government." Arendt opposes nation-state government, too, although not from the standpoint of the historical Kant, but, rather, from the standpoint of Brecht's "Pirate Jenny" and Friedrich Nietzsche's "Silenus." She is the criminal law-breaker, not the pro-feudalist, neo-Aristotelean lawmaker such as the Romantics Kant, Hegel, and Savigny. Thus, Arendt adopts the irrationalist, neo-Aristotelean logic of feudal law-maker Kant, as license for her own role as inveterate, anti-social law-breaker. There lie her own and her lover Heidegger's special affinities for the same kind of rabid irrationalism expressed by the very worst among the Nazis, as expressed similarly by today's radical "ecologists."

I repeat: the difference lies in the distinction between the same Thrasymachus as, on one occasion, playing the part of the mere criminal, and, on the next occasion, as a practicer of the legalized crime of an overlord. That changeling Thrasymachus, is incarnated as a pack of wolves one day, and the lord's pack of hounds, the next; whatever his role, it is never actually a human one. Between overlord and criminal,

---

22. See Leibniz on Locke, "New Essays on Human Understanding." See P. Valenti on the Leibniz-Locke controversy, "The Anti-Newtonian Roots of the American Revolution," ***Executive Intelligence Review***, Dec. 1, 1995. The Hitler-like quality of evil in Locke is reflected in the adoption of Locke as the official philosophy of treasonous Jefferson Davis' Confederacy: the notion of man as property. Locke is the antithesis of both the 1776 U.S. Declaration of Independence, and the Preamble for the 1789 U.S. Federal Constitution. Every U.S. patriot is the avowed enemy of Locke, or else he is no patriot, nor even decent person. Locke belongs in the same Hell with Arendt, Jean-Paul Sartre, and Adolf Hitler.

23. (Regensburg: Druck und Verlag Josef Habbel, 1952).

there is but one point of difference. Both are predators, preying upon mankind: one as lord, the other as outlaw. It is simply a matter of who is in power, butchering from within the castle, and who is attacking from outside. Both are self-defined as irrational beasts, as Arendt, Jaspers, and Heidegger define themselves as feral criminals; whereas Kant, as a parody of *The Republic*'s Glaucon, represents philosophical irrationalism *from a different social, political, and methodological standpoint*, than Hannah "Silenus" Arendt.

Hold that thought in view for a moment longer; the distinction I make is a most substantial one. In Plato's *The Republic*, what is the systemic difference between the notions of law of, respectively, Thrasymachus and Glaucon? Is it not clear, that there is more of Glaucon's irrationalism, than Thrasymachus', in Kant, and more of Thrasymachus in Arendt? As Plato stresses, both Thrasymachus and Glaucon rely, ultimately, on the same occult principle of irrationalism; but, there is a difference between them. Arendt is right to find the common element of irrationalism linking Kant to his empiricist British friends; but, she oversimplifies the differences.

Put the same question in other terms. What, after all, is the difference between Arendt and such professed Hobbesians as the already fully bestialized, former U.S. Secretary of State Henry A. Kissinger?[24] Had everything said against reason, by Arendt, not been properly said, already, by Paolo Sarpi's Francis Bacon, Hobbes, and their followers John Locke and Bernard de Mandeville? Was Hobbes not already satanic enough? What purpose does Arendt serve by her special emphasis upon Kant?[25]

> **Kant's importance, in his time, for Arendt later, and for all of us today, is that he became a convert, from empiricism, to neo-Aristoteleanism. He makes the same apology for irrationalism as the empiricists, such as Hobbes, but he makes it in an Aristotelean form. There lies his special influence, the special significance of his "Critiques," the perniciousness of his influence, still today.**

The point of difference was pointed out by G.W.F. Hegel, who identified Kant as a neo-Aristotelean. (Why should he not? Hegel himself was a neo-Aristotelean, too.) Here lies the significance of Kant for Arendt. Kant's importance, in his time, for Arendt later, and for all of us today, is that he became a convert, from empiricism, to neo-Aristoteleanism. He makes the same apology for irrationalism as the empiricists, such as Hobbes, but he makes it in an Aristotelean form. There lies his special influence, the special significance of his *Critiques*, the perniciousness of his influence, still today.

A summary of the relevant pages from modern history makes the distinctions clear. To understand the formal differences between "Dionysus" Arendt's and "Apollo" Kant's advocacies of irrationalism, one must situate those matters in their respectively different historical settings. I have given this account, frequently, in earlier published locations, but it must be said, to put Kant's relevance for our discussion into focus, here.

Immediately following the sessions of the mid-Fifteenth-Century's great ecumenical Council of Florence, the Venice-led feudalist factions of Europe launched a major counteroffensive against the work of that Council, and against the emergence of the first modern nation-state, Louis XI's France, out of the radiating influence of that Council. The initial focus of the Venice-led attack was the targetting of Cardinal Nicholas of Cusa and his influence; this attack was steered by the neo-Aristoteleans of Padua, as typified by Pietro Pomponazzi and his student Cardinal Gasp-

---

24. Kissinger so characterized himself, and the British people, in a public address at London's Chatham House, on May 10, 1982.

25. It is sufficient that it be noted here, that the destruction of Christianity, and also Judaism, were the principal immediate objectives of these existentialists, as of Prince Philip's World Wildlife Fund and "world religion" projects more recently. Heidegger's association with Tübingen University's "Liberation Theology," and similar roles of Jaspers, and of Martin Buber (for Zionism), are notable. Notable is the fact, that

Heidegger was by no means the originator of the influence of Nietzschean existentialism corrupting nominally Catholic circles in Germany; that current was already established at the beginning of the present century. Arendt's emphasis upon Kant is not exceptional; it is neo-Aristotelean influences within the churches, which were the flank exploited by those existentialists in their efforts to eradicate Christianity. The issue for these existentialist anti-Christians and anti-Semites, as for His Royal Anti-Christianness Prince Philip's World Wildlife Fund and "world religion" projects, is to eradicate that Mosaic conception of man's nature which defines men and women as made in the image of the Creator. There lies the explicitly satanic feature central to the existentialism of Jaspers, Heidegger, Arendt, Sartre, et al.

aro Contarini. Venice's victory over the League of Cambrai, condemned all of Europe to a ferocious, Venice-led anti-Renaissance, to a virtual reign of inquisitional terror, imposed, first, by Padua's Aristoteleans, and then by Paolo Sarpi's Venice-spawned empiricists.

With the rise of the Anglo-Dutch monarchy to power, during the Eighteenth Century, the Enlightenment spawned by Sarpi's and Abbot Antonio Conti's empiricists, became the dominant political force within Europe, especially after those 1789-1815 events which transformed the leading nation of Europe, France, into a virtually British-occupied, third-rate power. The subsequent downfall of London's sometime ally, Metternich's Holy Alliance, established Anglo-Dutch empiricism as the intellectual force of evil to be beaten within Western civilization as a whole.

Originally, Immanuel Kant was apparently little more than a German-speaking British empiricist, a Leibniz-hating propagandist for David Hume. Over the course of the 1770s, Kant underwent a shift in loyalties; he distanced himself from the increasing emphasis upon British styles in "philosophical indifferentism" to be found in Hume's evolving empiricism.[26] In this setting, Kant undertook a restatement of the same anti-Leibniz dogma which he had uttered ritually in his earlier incarnation as a British empiricist, but, as Hegel quips, this time from a neo-Aristotelean, rather than a simplistically empiricist standpoint. Thus, Kant became the founder of what became known as early Nineteenth-Century "German Critical Philosophy," the environment of Kantian and neo-Kantian Romanticism, in which the mind of Karl Marx, for example, was shaped.

During the late Nineteenth Century, various currents of outright satanism spread from Britain, onto the continent of Europe, finding a suitable habitat in those Vienna-Bayreuth connections which produced the influence of Richard Wagner, Ernst Mach, Anton Bruckner, Sigmund Freud, and the frankly satanic, Vienna theosophist's publication, *Lucifer*. This was the environment which produced the Europe-wide cult of worship of the Emperor Tiberius as the anti-Christ, the theosophist revival of the Mithra cult, centered on the Alex

Muenthe's and Maxim Gorki's Isle of Capri.[27] This part played by Capri was auxiliary to that played by old Venice, and by that nearby Duino castle of Torre e Tasso, where Rilke sojourned, and where mathematician Ludwig Boltzmann died mysteriously.

This epidemic of theosophical satanism among high-ranking influentials throughout Europe, is complementary to those Nineteenth-Century English devotees of Venice, at Oxford and Cambridge, whom we associate with the origins of the British Fabian Society, with the long reign of Edward VII in his roles of Prince of Wales and later King, and the emergence of the Round Table circles of Milner, MacKinder, H.G. Wells, et al., as also the closely related circles of satanic figures such as Bertrand Russell and Aleister Crowley. This was a period, in which the ultra-decadent relics of Central Europe merged with high-ranking British degenerates, in seeking to bring about that kind of general, dionysiac destruction of the existing civilization which was demanded in the syphilitic rantings of Satan-worshipping philologist Friedrich Nietzsche.

The "Hitler Project," to give the Nazi phenomenon its most aptly descriptive title, was of a pair with Georg Lukacs and such of his spiritual offspring of the "Frankfurt School" collation as Adorno and Arendt. All were, together with Britain's Houston Stewart Chamberlain, of the same species as Oxford's ultra-kookish John Ruskin, and Aleister Crowley. Once one has pointed out the essential common feature of the Hitler Project and the Frankfurt School, its foundations in dionysiac lust for destruction of the existing society, and the "Frankfurt School's" influence in shaping the "march through the institutions of Germany" by the so-called "Sixty-Eighters," one has begun, at least, to understand the use which Arendt chooses to make of old I. Kant.

Today, the significance of Arendt's generation of

---

26. This point is stated most clearly within Kant's introduction to the first edition of his *Critique of Pure Reason*, and referenced with less precision in his *Prolegomena*.

27. The coalition for victory assembled by Octavian, later Augustus Caesar, over the forces of Antony and Cleopatra, was negotiated with representatives of the Mithra cult at the Isle of Capri. In consequence, the Isle of Capri remained the personal property of whoever was Emperor of Rome, until about A.D. 500, when the Byzantine Roman Emperor transferred the title to a monastic order. According to archive records made available to me, the order for the execution of Jesus Christ was issued, from Capri, by the Emperor Tiberius to his personal representative, the husband of Tiberius' ward, Pontius Pilate. Muenthe purchased the site of Tiberius' palace, from which he established Capri as the world-capital of Satanism and homosexuality for the early Twentieth Century.

"Frankfurt School" figures, is, that they provided the spores of a new cultural fungus which emerged during the post-World War II period, a new guise of satanism for the generation coming into adulthood during the 1960s and 1970s. This was the generation of university youth targetted for recruitment by the World Wildlife Fund of Britain's Prince Philip and the Netherlands' SS veteran, Prince Bernhard. As Prince Philip's circles have explained, this so-called "ecological" initiative, like related projects for establishing a paganist "world religion," was aimed at the destruction of civilization in the name of Satan herself, a.k.a. Gaea, Isis, Ishtar, Cybele, et al. Like the syphilitic Nietzsche, Arendt, Heidegger, et al., they, and such offspring of Philip's World Wildlife Fund as the Club of Rome, were committed to going beyond everything Hitler visibly intended, to the total destruction of not only Judeo-Christian civilization, but everything which suggested civilized life, all in the satanic name of "nature." For them, it was imperative to discredit the sterile formalism of Aristotle, almost as much as the creative genius represented by Plato.

Call the spawn of Prince Philip's enterprise "the post-Nietzscheans." This mephistophelean crew did not intend to reproduce a situation like that under Venice's neo-Aristoteleanism of the mid-Sixteenth Century feudal reaction, in which Aristotle was promoted as the philosopher of feudal conservatism, for the sake of defeating Plato's influence. The American Revolution, and the world-wide impact of U.S. President Abraham Lincoln's triumph over Lord Palmerston's British Empire, had unleashed a mood of maddened desperation among the circles of Britain's Palmerston-shaped Prince of Wales, later Edward VII. After the global impact of the industrial revolution launched from the U.S.A. during the 1861-1876 interval, Britain could not triumph over the American Revolution within the framework of capitalism as Lord Shelburne, Jeremy Bentham, and Lord Palmerston had defined it. The enraged circles of the Prince of Wales and his followers, such as the satanic trio of H.G. Wells, Aleister Crowley, and Bertrand Russell, could be satisfied by nothing less than such satanic orgies of pure destruction as Britain's launching of World War I, Hitler afterward, and the worse blight of today's "New Age" after that.

For these enraged royal relics, and their lackeys, of the Babylonian, Roman, and Venetian oligarchical legacy, it was deemed necessary to tear up the roots, to destroy almost everything, in an effort to establish a modern science-fictioneer's version of a global—perhaps even galactic—neo-feudalist, one-world empire. Britain's orchestration of the processes leading into World War I, was the first step. The satanic moods spread among demoralized, enraged recruits to the so-called "Frankfurt School," were, like the Nazis, typical of the next step toward chaos.

To understand the growth of Kant's influence within the Germany of the Eighteenth-Century, empiricist "Enlightenment," one must take into account the connection of pre-1783 France to Benjamin Franklin's American Revolution, and must understand Kant of the 1780s and 1790s in light of the combined impacts of the American and French revolutions. To understand the actual Kant, one must see the contrasting situation, after Kant's death, of Hegel and Savigny during the so-called "neo-Kantian period" following the Holy Alliance and the Metternichian Carlsbad decrees which defined Hegel as Prussia's "state philosopher." We must also take into account the entirely different, later, global circumstances of a period after the American victory of 1865, which shook, and threatened to totter London's world: a new situation developed, followed by the change in the world resulting from the successful assassination of U.S. President McKinley by British agents, in 1901, followed by two World Wars and their nuclear-age sequel.

The Immanuel Kant of the *Critiques*, belongs to a specific period of history, a period with its own characteristics, a period of different characteristics than the pre-1776 period of Kant's life and writings, and a period of different characteristics than that after 1815, that different than the world after 1865, that different than the world after that 1901 assassination of U.S. President McKinley, that different than the circumstances after 1918, and that different than the world after 1962-63.

Ideas can, and must be assessed in absolute, scientific terms, as they correspond, or fail to correspond, by crucial-experimental standards, to man's relationship to nature in general terms. However, to account for the processes in which these same ideas are developed, or not developed, how they become popular, or not, and how they interact with social processes, we must pay close attention to the specific circumstances of the social processes within which the spread of, and reaction to such ideas are defined.

In absolute terms, considering any idea as it may reemerge in different historical settings, Kant was, and remains the evil irrationalist which Arendt admires him as being; but he was not a creature of Arendt's time. When she recognizes his irrationalism as a precedent which modern existentialists have adopted for their own purposes, she is correct. Beyond that point, her scholarship was wildly in error.

Kant's ideas were chosen and deployed by him, in his place and time, with the intent to influence the social and political circumstances which Kant imagined to exist, either during his life, or what he might have envisaged as his life's immediate aftermath. Thus, abstractly, academically Arendt may appear to be right about Kant's irrationalism, but he would have rejected the overtly satanic, Twentieth-Century standpoint which she attributes to him, retrospectively.

Kant would have rejected her view, doing so on the authority, admittedly not of reason, but as an affront to the arbitrary authority of what he regarded, with considerable emphasis on this point, as the custom of his time, of the historic specificity of that custom. On this point, Hegel's division of history into successive periods ordered by a "World-Spirit," and Savigny's notion of *Volksgeist*, are relevant references for any representative of the "German Critical Philosophy," reflections of the kind of occult irrationalism common to all of the Romantics of the late Eighteenth through mid-Nineteenth Centuries. From the standpoint of Romantics such as Kant and Hegel, Arendt belongs to a different time, expresses a *Volksgeist* of a different, nihilist age, the "New Age," an age of destructive perversion for its own sake.

Nonetheless, hers could not be popularly regarded as an unusual error among the classroom customs of these present, degenerate times of academic "speech codes," when perversion for its own sake runs amok. The revival of pro-Kantian apologetics during the post-1918 period, belongs not to Kantianism—the Age of Pisces, but to the age of satanism—the Age of Aquarius, to a time when Arendt dragged Kant's literary corpse out of that poor wretch's grave; it was her necromancy which called up his rotting old bones, to clatter

Sometimes, it is indispensable to view a stubbornly fixed strain of culture in the man, as an entomologist might study the apparently instinctive, fixed "opinion-making" behavior of a species of bug. As a species, or variety, the bug-in-itself, such as the philosophy of Kant's "Critiques," or of existentialists, resists those changes in its nature by means of which it might prosper as a type. This resistance to change—to healthy directions of self-development—constitutes its bug-likeness, the quality which sets it outside the domain of human nature.

them, to serve the cause of contemporary satanism. The satanism which Arendt and her co-thinkers impute to Kant, is nothing other than what they have chosen to attribute to his remains, when he is no longer in a position to protest.

Sometimes, it is indispensable to view a stubbornly fixed strain of culture in the man, as an entomologist might study the apparently instinctive, fixed "opinion-making" behavior of a species of bug. As a species, or variety, the bug-in-itself, such as the philosophy of Kant's *Critiques*, or of existentialists, resists those changes in its nature by means of which it might prosper as a type. This resistance to change—to healthy directions of self-development—constitutes its bug-likeness, the quality which sets it outside the domain of human nature.

The lesson to be learned from the fact that the possibility, that such poisonous sophistries as those of either a Kant or an Arendt, could be accepted as customary opinion among widely influential strata, should remind us, that the biggest, worst, most self-destructive lies, are always those which have become accepted as customary opinion.

Again: Such a resistance to change of species-like axioms of behavior, should remind us, painfully, of the entomologist's experimental subject, the bug. It is always in the name of customary, or "popular" opinion, that nations and entire cultures perpetrate their worst crimes against humanity. Such bug-like cultures are eerily inhuman; they can not adapt to what is, for them, an alien reality; they prefer their pre-existing customs, even if these consign them to doom. A failed culture customarily blames its failures upon its toleration of beliefs and behaviors it considers alien to its custom; the ugly truth is, that it is a nation's thus bug-like adherence to its own pre-established, popular beliefs, not its unpopular ones, which condemns a society to a species-like kind of self-destruction.

The kind of existentialism which Arendt represents, is the worst, most pernicious form of popular opinion, under which the very worst crimes against humanity, are those actions most likely to be perpetrated. Remember, Nazism itself was nothing but a variant of the same type of existentialism which Arendt herself, like her sometime lover, and Nazi philosopher, Martin Heidegger, also represented. Remember, from comparing expressed public opinion in Germany, on the subject of Nazism, in 1932 and 1934, that popular opinion tells us less about what a people believes is truthful, than what the typical citizen thinks it prudent to be overheard believing.

Admittedly, existentialism of the Nazi and "Frankfurt School" varieties, is one of the relatively extreme forms of moral degeneracy; nor, prior to Hitler's appointment as Chancellor, was it prevailing belief in Germany. Yet, on account of the fact that it tends to exist only as an extreme and minority viewpoint, the spread of existentialism in Germany, during the 1920s and early 1930s, is all the more relevant as a subject of clinical investigation: it is the disease which spreads widely only in its most virulent forms. Yet, on just this account, we may cite the hopeful fable: "It is an ill wind that blows nobody good." It were better said by Leibniz: This is the best of all possible worlds, a world in which disgust for Voltaire may promote otherwise neglected virtues. The evil which Arendt represents, points our attention to the perniciousness with which the contemporary, prevailing tyranny of "Big Brother," of public opinion, threatens the continued existence of civilization today. The stagnation and suppression of economic science by today's New Age fads, may prompt the immune reaction which destroys the fads' influence. The induced influence of expressed public opinion and matching bad taste, in Germany then, or the U.S.A. today, is an excellent, and most relevant case of a type of evil which may, with some help from us, bring about the conditions for its own doom.

The existentialist is, thus, like a species of bug, clinging hysterically to fixed patterns of ostensibly "instinctive" behavior; therein lies its vulnerability, *on condition that we exploit that vulnerability.* The Kantian is a higher form of life than existentialists such as Arendt, but also avows the same fatal, bug-like quality of irrationalism, of customary cognitive sterility. The

> **These, Kantians or existentialists, are abnormal, defective cultural strains, which have suppressed in themselves those qualities for adaptation which distinguish the human species from the bug-in-itself. These are creatures which have chosen to reject what is rightly called "human nature," the nature of a creature made in the image of the Creator.**

same vulnerability inheres in today's devotees of "post-industrial" utopia, of "free trade," and "globalization." These, Kantians or existentialists, are abnormal, defective cultural strains, which have suppressed in themselves those qualities for adaptation which distinguish the human species from the bug-in-itself. These are creatures which have chosen to reject what is rightly called "human nature," the nature of a creature made in the image of the Creator. Since they, although victims of such degraded customs, are, nonetheless human, they have qualities by means of which their culture might choose to survive in a better form; if they refuse that choice, the mechanisms of opinion which cause them to reject that choice, to rather cling to fatal habits of opinion-making, demonstrate that these habits are pathologies in the same sense as a cancer, or other ostensibly terminal disease of living tissue.

Science and Human Nature

The essence of physical science, is that the individual human being is distinguished from all other species, by those willfully developable qualities of creative mentation, which account for the generation of all validated discoveries of efficiently applicable physical principle, and also principles of Classical artistic composition. The human individual is not naturally bug-like, nor like any lower form of life; culturally decadent, or not, he represents no type of species but, at worst, a morally sick man.

This fact of actual human nature, has always been in direct, and irreconcilable opposition to any social order in which one set of persons, as oligarchs and their lackeys, hold, usually, a larger number of other people in the status of virtual human cattle. Once it is admitted to be a fact of natural law, that truth exists for man, only as mankind discovers, proves, and adopts principles by means of this creative mental faculty, then it should be clear, that no notion of social order *should* be tolerated which conflicts with that scientific proof of the universal nature of the human individual. Nonetheless, all persons who have chosen to be either oligarchs, or oligarchs' lackeys, will abhor, and seek to suppress, as the London-directed, evil conspirators behind the short-lived U.S. Confederacy did, any body of practice which is viewed as a threat to the social relations premised upon holding some people as virtual human cattle.

As we have indicated, a moment ago, in referring to 1920s and 1930s existentialism as largely a superimposed belief: oligarchs and their lackeys can not establish durable tyrannies, merely by force applied from above. Such force will have a durable effect, only if it is tolerated by the corruption of the oppressed themselves.

In effect, durable tyrannies are those Orwellian tyrannies, in which the ruled put their rulers' shackles on not only their own minds, but those of their neighbors, each morning upon arising. To induce a man to accept degradation to the status of a chicken or a cow, you must induce him to risk much to defend, as his imagined self-interest, that status and culture of which he believes to be the natural rights of such a chicken or cow. A successful tyranny is one in which the culturally acquired instinct of induced popular opinion, impels the victim to defend the system of tyranny within which he lives; even in those same moments he complains of the behavior of the tyrant, he will demand, even forcefully, that his fellow-victim not disturb the arrangement with the oppressor. A successful tyranny is one the victim is loathe to escape, lest he might lose the hard-won real or imagined benefits he believes himself to have gained under the rules of that regime. The empiricists' notion of a democratic "social contract" typifies such cupidity of such victims.

These rules defining the tyrants' relatively successful, or unsuccessful manipulation of virtual human cattle, are not mere generalities. These reflect deep principles, scientific principles, underlying such pathetic behavior by such apparently willing victims. These considerations go to the heart of the topic we identified at the outset of this report.

Those considerations are of two types. First, they are derived directly from the fundamental principle of economic science itself. Second, they express the way in which a pathological misapplication of the principles of that science, whether by intent, or otherwise, may induce chicken-like or cow-like tendencies for submission among the relevant virtual human cattle. The way in which populations of prospective science-graduates are "brainwashed" by fear of losing their standing according to the rules of "generally accepted classroom mathematics," illustrates both types of considerations

in a single case.

That said, now let us describe the science which provides us the alternative.

I have repeatedly stated the principled features of my discoveries, including repeated references supplied in recently published locations. Therefore, in this present instance, it were timely, sufficient, and would help the readers' concentration on the specific topic at hand here, to summarize, once again, the principled features of my discoveries in physical economy, and related principles of human nature, point by point.

1. The Structure of Conscious Creative Mentation

The architecture of the conscious thought of an individual's cognitively cultivated mind, may be defined summarily as follows.

a. The *primary* individual elements of such conscious thought are principles, such as validated individual physical principles. These principles are of two meaningfully distinguished types, physical principles and principles of Classical artistic composition in art, the latter defined as generated and interacting in the same type of manner as physical principles.

b. These principles form a multiply-connected, hypergeometric manifold, in the sense that Carl Gauss and Bernhard Riemann define such manifolds. Within such a manifold, each element interacts with other elements in the same way Johannes Kepler defines the interactions among planetary orbits, as located *primarily* in the interactions among the entire array of orbits as such (rather than orbits being defined as products of action-at-a-distance among individual bodies within the system as a whole). I designate the presently *implicitly* known number of physical principles by the conventional symbolic number "n," and the corresponding number of principles of Classical artistic composition by the symbolic number "m." Combined, and interacting, these define a multiply-connected manifold, of implicitly Riemannian form, "n+m."

An apt choice of example of the form of action in such a manifold, is the type of motivic thorough-composition developed successively by Joseph Haydn, Wolfgang Mozart, Ludwig van Beethoven, et al., on the basis of those notions of well-tempered polyphony and counterpoint derived from the work of J.S. Bach. Bach's *A Musical Offering*, which provided Mozart the most crucial starting-point of reference for this method of motivic thorough-composition, is one benchmark for this development. The principles of inversion presented by Bach's **The Art of the Fugue**, as examined by Beethoven, represent another crucial benchmark for understanding this method of polyphonic composition. Crucial is, that all actually heard and otherwise implied voices in the composition, interact in the same sense Kepler defines the interactions among planetary orbits as such.

The same principled character of Classical artistic composition, is exhibited by Classical poetry, from which Classical musical composition is entirely derived, and in the thorough-composition of Classical Greek tragedy, and the tragedies developed by Shakespeare and Schiller in modern times.[28]

2. The Content 0f Principles

The content of each principle in such a manifold, is provided by the mode in which validatable discoveries of universal principle are generated by the perfectly sovereign cognitive processes of the individual human mind. The definition of each principle is associated with three steps:

a. The existence, in reality, of an undeniable inconsistency, or incoherence, for which no formal solution exists in terms of previously established principles.[29]

b. The generation of a tentative solution, a solution stated in the form of a discovered new principle, a mental act occurring only within the sovereign precincts of the individual's cognitive processes, a mental action which can not be communicated as information, but whose replication can be induced, with more or less great precision, within other sovereign individual minds.

c. The rigorous experimental form of validation of the newly discovered principle.

The relevant act of discovery of a new principle, occurs through what is more easily recognized after the fact, as the "mental energy" of concentration, out of which the validated solution was generated (or, the discovery was reexperienced, as by a student). This "mental energy" is of the quality associated with the use of the Platonic form of the Classical Greek term

agapē, as by Plato's Socrates, in Book II of **The Republic**, and as by the Apostle Paul in **I Corinthians** 13. It is most fairly described as that *passion for truth and justice* associated with the experiencing of a discovery of validatable physical or Classical-artistic principle.[30]

This quality of passion is associated with the Socratic method of Plato's dialogues, and with the reflection of that same method in the Schiller-Humboldt policy of Classical-humanist modes of education. This quality of passion, *agapē*, is intrinsic to creative discovery of validated physical principle; it is the quality of passion which provides the substance of Classical artistic forms of composition and performance.[31]

This quality of passion, so defined, is the empirical actuality of the individual cognitive processes which sets the human individual absolutely apart from, and above all animal species. This is the elementary expression of what is rightly termed *human nature*, as distinguished from the nature of any and all animals.

3. Learning Is Not Knowing

The act of knowing, as distinct from mere learning, occurs only in the form I have described for the act of validatable discovery of principle, above. In other words, we should condemn, as fraudulent, any program of education, which teaches "information," rather than requiring the student to relive the experience of generating for what is, for that student, an original discovery of a new, validatable, physical or Classical-artistic type of principle.

Thus, in the Classical-humanist mode of education, the student learns virtually nothing other than reliving, within the sovereign processes of the student's own cognitive processes, a large number of physical and artistic principles, one by one, using, in each instance, the three-step method of cognition which I have indicated above.

In this educational process, whether in classroom or private study, the student accumulates a justified sense of certainty (e.g., truthfulness) of a number of principles. This accumulation of principles forms a kind of lattice-work, reflecting thus the fact that every new principle acquired so, has been generated as a validatable solution for paradoxes posed in respect to previ-

---

28. The notable opposition to these views on music and tragedy is typified by the cases of the proto-Nazi existentialists Richard Wagner and Friedrich Nietzsche. Typical of Nietzsche's Romantic irrationalism, is his infantile assertion that music is rooted in the dance. On such matters of art, Nietzsche amuses himself by ridiculing Kant, but fears and hates Friedrich Schiller.

29. e.g., a Classical metaphor.

---

30. In this Platonic usage, "justice" signifies a solution consistent with fostering the development of the truth-seeking cognitive powers of all human individuals.

31. Lyndon H. LaRouche, Jr., "The Substance of Morality," **Executive Intelligence Review**, June 26, 1998.

ously mastered principles. This functionally integrated "lattice-work" represents, then, the student's *knowledge* at any point in the individual's educational and related development.

That brings us to something of far more importance to be said on this matter. The experience of generating this lattice-work of cumulatively known principles, is the student's growing intimacy with his, or her own creative mental processes. This experience has two types of features, each feature interacting with the other, both always interdependent.

a. The lattice is of the quality of a multiply-connected manifold, such that the entirety of that interacting, interdependent array is acting, as a unified intellectual force, on each problem to which it is summoned.[32] The efficient connection among principles, which permits this lattice to function as a multiply-connected manifold, is established only through the generation of each known principle in a Classical-humanist or equivalent mode.

b. The principle of action, by means of which the solution to the paradox is generated, is not an object of the senses, and can neither be known as, nor represented as if it were an object of the senses. It is known only as a mental object, an object of the process of generating cognitive solutions (discoveries of principle) for well-defined paradoxes.[33] However, otherwise, this principle of creative mental action becomes better known, more reliable, through experience. The relevant

quality of experience required for this effect, is the experience of expanding the lattice-work of principles through methods equivalent to the Classical-humanist mode of education.

This form of education is also to be regarded as moral education. "Moral" does not signify shibboleths, a list of "do's" and "don'ts." As the Apostle Paul condemns the Pharisaical moralists, in ***I Corinthians*** 13, moral instruction means nothing other than *agapē*: the quality of passion which drives one relentlessly to seek out truth and justice in all matters. "I never claim to know anything, when I have merely learned it as 'information,' or by simple personal experience." I must know it according to the standard of truthfulness and justice associated with validated cognitive knowledge of principle. That, and that alone, is moral education; only a Classical-humanist mode of education, is a moral education. Other forms of education, are immoral, since they are governed by no human principle of relentless commitment to scientific truthfulness.

4. The Function of Classical Artistic Composition

Most people today are morally defective by virtue of their induced, moral and intellectual "littleness," their selfishness, their lack of the equivalent of a Classical-humanist mode of education. In consequence of their ignorance, most people locate their idea of self-interest as did those Nineteenth-Century **wretches** called "Scottish moral philosophers," such as David Hume and Adam Smith. In the words of the Smith thus self-described as morally degenerate:

"The administration of the great system of the universe … the care of the universal happiness of all rational and sensible beings, is the business of God and not of man. To man is allotted a much humbler department, but one much more suitable to the weakness of his powers, and to the narrowness of his comprehension: the care of his own happiness, of that of his family, his friends, his country…. But though we are … endowed with a very strong desire of those ends, it has been intrusted to the slow and uncertain determinations of our reason to find out the proper means of bringing them about. Nature has directed us to the greater part of these by *original and immediate instincts. Hunger, thirst, the passion which unites the two sexes, the love of pleasure, and the*

---

32. Contrary to a widespread delusion, neither "fractals" nor "random number theory" define the meaning of "non-linear." The first approximation of the notion of true "non-linearity," is found in the results of the attempt to map a spherical surface, for example, simply to a plane surface. The treatment of the so-called five Platonic solids by Plato's Academy, is an example of this. Nicholas of Cusa's definition of a circle as of a higher order of cardinality than irrational numbers, points to that same issue, as does the work on Platonic solids by such Cusa followers as Pacioli, Leonardo, and Kepler. The more general expression of "non-linearity" is associated with the Kepler-Leibniz-Gauss-Riemann hypergeometries of true multiply-connected manifolds, for which, in every case the characteristic action in the infinitesimally small is always non-linear. The latter is the fact which discredits axiomatically Augustin Cauchy's limit theorem.

33. Physical reality is not located in the individual sense-perception as such, but, rather, in those changes in human mental behavior which result in the increase of mankind's power over nature (e.g., reproducible potential relative population-density) per capita and per square kilometer of the Earth's surface. It is the type of mental action which generates results in this direction which is the physical reality of cognitive experience, as distinct from the false notion of "physical reality" associated with Aristotelean or other merely contemplative views of individual sense-perceptions.

dread of pain, prompt us to apply these means for their own sakes, and without any consideration of their tendency to those beneficent ends which the great Director of nature intended to produce by them."[34]

What Smith so describes, is a crude superstition, an echo of his predecessor, the satanic Bernard de Mandeville. Like Hume, Smith's little man relies upon what he asserts to be an unknowable principle, a principle alleged to be producing wonderful effects by some means, and in some way inaccessible to his own comprehension. That means is known to him only as the "hedonistic principle" of Thomas Hobbes et al. Thus, Smith and all of his followers define themselves as lunatics, as superstitious, heathen worshippers of an occult statistical principle. The same "hedonistic principle" is otherwise familiar from Thomas Hobbes, John Locke, from Mandeville's *The Fable of the Bees,*[35] or from Jeremy Bentham's *Introduction to the Principles of Morals and Legislation.*[36]

The source of the influence of the wicked superstition of a Mandeville, an Adam Smith, a Friedrich von Hayek, or a Milton Friedman, lies within the personal moral depravity of the person who believes such trash as Smith's. Such depraved, e.g., empiricist, belief, is motivated by passions of a quality directly opposite to *agapē,* by those piggish passions, such as those of Sir Henry A. Kissinger's May 10, 1982 Chatham House address, rooted in the Hobbesian's particular sense-impressions, rather than cognitive judgment. These are people whose motivating, morbid misconception of personal self-interest corresponds to nothing which is not essentially perverse and bestial.

This point is best demonstrated from the vantage-point of those principles of Classical-humanist education we have referenced above. The lattice-work of principles defined by such a method of education, defines the relationship between a student and an original discoverer, as implicitly a relationship located within what philosophers have defined as a simultaneity of eternity: the student lives in the discoverer's time, and the original discoverer's moment of creative thought lives still, and that efficiently, in the present time, through the student. Nothing occult is assumed; everything is comprehensible. Two crucial moral principles are illustrated by that example. First, our present relationship to past and future, exists in terms of our cognitive generation, and regeneration, of those ideas which correspond to validated discoveries of principle. Second, our personal, world-historical identity exists, morally, in our present, *cognitive* connection to both that past and that future.

How, then, should we view the person who defines his notion of personal self-interest, and corresponding motivation, as Smith prescribes? That person is a caricature of a human being, a rutting Yahoo, with the outward form of a human being, but the morals of a monkey masturbating publicly, in the cage at the zoo. Ah! But we are rebuked, "But, that is the way that man chooses, freely, to define his self-interest!" Who are we, to be so tasteless, as to question the opinion of a man who makes a monkey of himself?

We must see the moral implications of a Classical-humanist form of education from this standpoint. It is only through replicating the validatable discoveries of principle from the past, and defining our relationship to the future in that same perspective, that an individual has a conscious, efficient, and general relationship to both past and future members of humanity. Only through that kind of efficient and conscious social relationship, can the individual define a rational notion of personal self-interest. Furthermore, it is only as the individual recognizes the essential social relations to be of this form, that that individual is capable of a sane definition of his, or her own identity. Otherwise, in functional terms, he or she is no better than a poor *Golem,* with no soul.

Here lies the essence of Classical artistic composition.

Our portrait of the individual human mind, locates the essence of the human personality within the sovereign bounds of those cognitive processes in which insights into validatable solutions for ontological paradoxes are generated. No direct communication, as by gestures, language, and so on, between such sovereign processes of one individual, and the same quality of sovereign processes of another, is possible. As the impending bankruptcy of the Internet's hyperinflated financial bubble, will soon illustrate that point, no cogni-

---

34. emphasis added. Adam Smith, *The Theory of Moral Sentiments.* The passage is as quoted in Lyndon H. LaRouche, Jr. and David P. Goldman, *The Ugly Truth About Milton Friedman* (New York: New Benjamin Franklin House, 1980), p. 107.

35. Bernard Mandeville, *The Fable of the Bees, or Private Vices, Public Benefits* (London: 1934, reprint of 1714 edition).

36. Jeremy Bentham, *Introduction to the Principles of Morals and Legislation* (Buffalo, N.Y.: Prometheus Books, 1988).

tive, productive communication in the form of mere so-called "information" is possible.

Nonetheless, we can induce such a state of discovery of principle, which has occurred within our own mind, within another person's. We do this, by appropriate forms of prompting action, prompting the other person to undergo the same creative process we have experienced within our own mind. That Socratic type of prompting action is typified, by the polemical methods of Classical-humanist education.

Thus, the class of actions associated with the replication of the act of a validatable discovery of principle, is the most important, and the only distinctively human form of transaction among human individuals. Any behavior which is controllable by methods of drill and grill, or other mere learning, is not human in and of itself, although it might be, in some particular instances, a necessary auxiliary to an actually human form of action. Thus, the most essential relations among persons, are those which pertain to those modes of indirect communication effected by inducing replications of sovereign cognitive experiences, as we do in successful application of methods of Classical-humanist education. In general, we may say of this, that the power to prompt others to generate what are, for them, validatable discoveries of principle, is the only essentially human form of relationship, the form of relationship which pertains most directly to that human identity which is located, for each individual, within the set of relations pertaining to the simultaneity of eternity.

This special quality of relationship, among individuals' respectively sovereign cognitive processes, is an impassioned relationship. The passion is of that quality we have associated with *agapē*. This quality of passion is pivotted on those issues of truth and justice which pertain to principles, such as physical principles, but also the principles associated with Classical forms of artistic composition.

However, the passion involved is concerned with not merely the physical principles governing the individual's interaction with the universe. The primary concern is communicable insight into the workings of the minds of other human beings: in other words, artistic principles. The ability to conceptualize such insights, within the sovereign cognitive processes of other individuals, and to provoke thus their intended effect, as communication of principled ideas, provides the essential integument among individual persons, without which mankind's physical relationship to the universe

could not be an anti-entropic one.

The entirety of art, so viewed, depends absolutely upon an underlying and overriding commitment to truth and justice—motivation by the passion of *agapē*. Nothing false can be decently described as art; no form of artistic composition which is not governed pervasively by a commitment to say nothing which is not true *in principle* deserves the dignity of being treated as art.

5. History as Science

A reflective study of Classical tragedy, as the tragedies of Aeschylus, Sophocles, Marlowe, Shakespeare, and Schiller best typify the medium, taken together,[37] shows us a direct connection between Classical artistic composition and history. Think of the mastery of the subject of history as a Classical art-form. Incorporate within the domain of this art-form, the subjects of physical science in general, and physical economy in particular.

Putting these together in this multiply-connected way, we have all of the aspects of statecraft incorporated under history, and history subsumed by the notion of Classical artistic composition in general. So viewed, and so practiced, the competent mastery of the subject of history, is a product of Classical artistry, which is also science in the strictest meaning of the latter term.

6. The Machine-Tool Principle

For the modern science graduate, oriented to experience with both pedagogical and research experiments, the general idea of a machine-tool principle is perhaps a bit too obvious. As an integral part of his 1792-1794 revolution in warfare, Lazare Carnot introduced his principle of machine-tool design to forced-draft mass- and series-production of weaponry and other relevant impedimenta of warfare and its logistics. These principles were introduced into the U.S.A., beginning 1814, by collaborators of the circles of Carnot and Gaspard Monge. These principles were adopted as a central feature of the U.S. West Point Military Academy, and engineers educated by West Point established the foundations for what became the U.S. agro-industrial revolution of 1861-1876. Thus, the machine-tool industry was born, and given its initial development.

That U.S. industrial revolution, copied by Germany,

---

37. And these also taken together with the Classical (satirical) comedy of a Euripides, Boccaccio, François Rabelais, Miguel Cervantes' ***Don Quixote***, and Shakespeare.

A machinist checks the dimensions of a part for a walking dragline. "The principles of machine-tool design developed by Lazare Carnot, were introduced into the United States in 1814. Engineers trained in these principles at West Point Military Academy established the foundations for what became the U.S. agro-industrial revolution of 1861-1876. Thus, the machine-tool industry born, and given its initial development."

Russia, Japan, and other nations, beginning the late 1870s, has been responsible for all of the leading economic achievements of modern industrial development.

From this simpler picture of the process, the connections involved are represented by three successive steps, these including the same process of discovery to which we referred earlier, here. First, there is the paradox which leads to the discovery of a (for example) new physical principle. Second, an apparatus must be designed which provides crucial-experimental tests of the validity of this assumed discovery. Thirdly, from the refined design of such a successful crucial-experimental

apparatus, we adduce principles of application of the discovered principle, principles of application we call "technologies," applied to designs of products and productive processes.

In its broader terms, as Lazare Carnot first elaborated the principles of machine-tool design,[38] he revolutionized the notion of modern economy, picking up from where Leibniz's continuing work on the general principle of heat-powered machinery was interrupted, in effect, only by Leibniz's death. After Carnot, the notion of industrial progress in design of products and productive processes, must trace the origins and application of technological progress from a Classical-humanist approach to education (Carnot's Oratorian-shaped approach to the principles of education), through crucial-experimental proof of principle, through the refinement of the application of the principle according to considerations of design of heat-powered machines, and to the improved design of products and production processes.

Carnot's work carries the principles of the American System of political-economy beyond U.S. Treasury Secretary Alexander Hamilton's emphasis upon "artificial labor," to an implied set of inequalities governing policies for school-leaving age, levels of household culture, increasing roles of pedagogical and research laboratories and experiments, and the increasing weight of a machine-tool-design industry, as such, within the total division of labor within production, physical distribution, and basic economic infrastructure's development and maintenance.

After the successive work of Leibniz, Benjamin Franklin, Hamilton, and Carnot, in launching the industrial revolution, these principles of division of labor in education, research, machine-tool design, and output-ratios generally, are the foundation for any competent education of economists, engineers, and industrial

---

38. Lazare Carnot, "Essai sur les machines en général" (Essay on Machines in General), 1738. See Dino De Paoli's Nov. 21, 1998 address to a conference of the Schiller Institute at Bad Schwalbach, Germany, on Carnot's development of principles of machine-tool design, "Carnot's Theory of Technology as the Basis for Physical Economy" (to be published in a forthcoming issue of *EIR*). For a more refined insight into Carnot's work on machine-tool design, it is virtually indispensable to see the connections to Carnot's work on military fortification, as a generalization of the Leibnizian principle of "geometry of position" (i.e., *analysis situs*): Lazare Carnot, *De la défense des places fortes*, (Paris: Mme. DeCourcier, Libraire pour les mathématiques, 1812); the work was also translated into English in 1814 as, ***Treatise on the Defense of Fortified Places***.

management in the modern world.

When we turn our attention to some of the implications of such experimentation, matters are not quite so simple as a first glance at Carnot's work might suggest to the unwary. For our purposes here, we are obliged to focus on the apparent subtleties lurking behind what might seem the more obvious. We shall identify the nature of these deeper implications, now, and indicate their relevance for national economic policies, under the rubric of "anti-entropy," in the next-following section of this report.

To understand the underlying implications of Lazare Carnot's discovery and development of that machine-tool principle upon which the success of modern industrial economy depended absolutely, we must think of "energy" as Lazare and Sadi Carnot thought of "energy," not the reductionist hand-waving offered by Clausius, Grassmann, Kelvin, Rayleigh, et al., later during the Nineteenth Century. To define the mental framework within which the economist's understanding of the machine-tool principle must be situated, we must view the crucial, distinct contributions of both Lazare Carnot and of Carl Gauss from the standpoint of Kepler, as Leibniz's notion of the Kepler calculus, and of the related notions of *analysis situs,* bear on the distinct but complementary contributions of Lazare Carnot and Gauss.

For the scientifically literate popular reader, the best currently available pedagogical introduction to the point now to be made, is provided by a special, Summer 1998 issue of the quarterly **Fidelio**. That publication features the collaboration of Dr. Jonathan Tennenbaum and Bruce Director, "How Gauss Determined the Orbit of Ceres."[39] Here, we shall summarize the bearing upon the machine-tool principle, relying, for purposes of relative brevity, largely upon referring the reader to that pedagogical exercise for further background.

As we indicated here earlier, the distinctive ideas about geometry which emerged from among the best scientific minds of the Nineteenth Century, began with Classical Greek attention to the implications of attempting to map a spherical, or spheroidal surface simply to a plane surface. This problem was posed, from Classical Greek times, through the Nineteenth Century, by the functional interdependency between astrophysical and geodetic problems of mapping, including the interrelated problems of oceanic naviga-

tion. In Classical Greek times, the high-point of this line of investigation into geometry, was the subject of the five Platonic solids. It was at that point in the continuing investigation of such matters, with the launching of modern experimental physical science by Nicholas of Cusa, that modern science began. This standpoint in the work of Cusa, as explored further by such as Pacioli and Leonardo, brought science to the first effort to establish a general mathematical physics, the work of Johannes Kepler.

However, although all sensitive scientific thinkers recognized that the notion of geometry must not be based upon what the modern classroom often calls a Cartesian manifold, modern physics continued to be plagued by the generally accepted, superstitious classroom belief, belief in a merely conjectural, occult universe, in which elementary forms of action in space and time, moved, primitively, infinitely, and infinitesimally, in perfect straight-line action. It was not until Gauss follower Bernhard Riemann's restatement of the case for non-Euclidean geometry, in his 1854 habilitation dissertation, that arbitrary, axiomatically linear, notions of elementary space, time, and matter, were officially, sweepingly, and openly outlawed by a leading, influential scientific thinker.

Even today, most thinking about physical science, especially popularized opinions on these matters, clings to the Seventeenth-Century axiomatic superstitions of the Cartesians. The characteristic expression of such superstition, from Newton through Euler, to modern charlatans such as Bertrand Russell, Norbert ("information theory") Wiener, and John ("systems analysis") von Neumann, is the so-called principle of Augustin Cauchy's "limit theorem," the occult presumption, as by Leonhard Euler, that physical action in the universe is axiomatically linear in the infinitesimally small. Virtually all generally taught classroom economics is premised, still today, upon those same barbaric superstitions. In most of today's university economics classrooms and business schools, the same Cartesian delusions of Isaac Newton, are worshipped as Dr. Samuel ("Samiel") Clarke's god, who, from time to time, winds up the universe.

In this immediate location, our attention is limited to one aspect of the contemporary problems caused by such Cartesian and related superstitions of the academic classroom: the issues bearing immediately on the economic principles immediately associated with the machine-tool principle and its application. As the

---

39. *Fidelio*, Summer 1998.

reader will discover, we address this problem with emphasis on the importance of a recent, Earth-shaking policy declaration, delivered at Russia's famous Novosibirsk science-city, by China's President Jiang Zemin.

Kepler's discovery, that the orbit of Mars was elliptical, rather than circular, led him, and his follower Leibniz, to recognizing the general problem of adducing the non-constant trajectories of celestial bodies, from relatively infinitesimal observed intervals of those bodies' trajectories. This challenge defined the need for the development of what became Leibniz's calculus. This is the same challenge addressed by Gauss, in discovering that the orbit of Ceres was of the same characteristics which Kepler had already assigned to a missing planet of the Solar system, whose orbit lay between those of Mars and Jupiter.[40]

The entire sweep of Kepler's work, through his *The New Astronomy*,[41] was dominated by Kepler's recognition that there was a relationship between the ordering of the Solar system's orbits, and the internal ordering of the five Platonic solids as a series. This standpoint Kepler never abandoned, contrary to some commentators who have argued, groundlessly, that this standpoint was abandoned at a later point. This view of the Solar system as such a system, is underlined by two features of Kepler's later progress: 1) The emphasis upon the harmonic characteristics of the elliptical orbits, relative to a common Solar focus; 2) That Kepler himself did not fall into the fatal three-body paradox of Newton's effort to reinvent "Kepler's Three Laws" from the fallacious standpoint of Galileo's empiricist, "action at a distance" hoax. Kepler emphasized that the orbits of the planets interacted as orbits, not as trajectories determined by action-at-a-distance forces among individual orbiting bodies.

Thus, already, Kepler's astrophysics was based on that notion of a hypergeometric, multiply-connected manifold, of the type later developed, successively, by Gauss and Riemann. Leibniz's development of a calculus in which the infinitesimal interval of characteristic action of a trajectory is intrinsically one of non-constant curvature (i.e., axiomatically non-linear), is derived from examination of the implications of just such a Kepler-Gauss-Riemann development of hypergeo-

metric, multiply-connected manifolds.[42]

Since Lazare Carnot's treatment of the geometry of position, did not extend treatment of Leibniz's design for a calculus of the infinitesimally small interval of action, to the scope of Gauss's and Riemann's later work on *analysis situs,* Carnot's development of the machine-tool principle remains only an extremely fruitful approximation, until the considerations added by Gauss and Riemann are taken into account. To generalize the principles of machine-tool design to the degree needed for today's applications to physical economy in general, the Gauss-Riemann work on physical geometries of Keplerian multiply-connected manifolds, must be added.

21st Century Science & Technology and Germany's *Fusion* magazine have pursued an exemplary demonstration of the significance of what I have just said, in their presentation of the work of Gauss and his collaborator Wilhelm Weber on the subject of the Ampère angular electrodynamic force measured by Weber, and willfully ignored by Maxwell.[43] In connection with the point, on the principles of machine-tool

---

40. Tennenbaum and Director, op. cit.

41. Johannes Kepler, *New Astronomy,* trans. by W.H. Donahue (Cambridge, U.K.: Cambridge University Press, 1992).

42. One must judge thus the merits of Abbot Antonio Conti's, Samuel Clarke's, and Isaac Newton's claim, that Newton had developed a calculus independently of, and prior to Leibniz. First, Newton never claimed to have discovered a method which has any similarity to a calculus of the characteristics just described, above. Second, the attempt to defend Newton's worthless claim, as against Leibniz, has always been based on the purely superstitious assumption of the empiricists, of Euler, of Cauchy's "limit theorem," et al., that an infinitesimal interval of a functional trajectory is either intrinsically linear, or may be treated as linear. It was Descartes enthusiast Antonio Conti's insistence that elementary action in the universe must be linear in the infinitesimally small, which was the hoax employed to argue that Newton's fiddling with simple infinite series formed the basis for a calculus. This was also the basis for the hoax concocted by the Newton follower Euler, later, in his attacks on Leibniz's calculus of non-constant curvatures. In any actual calculus, that of a hypergeometric (multiply-connected manifold) domain, such as the Kepler-Gauss Solar system, the characteristic interval of action of a trajectory is always of intrinsically non-constant curvature (i.e., categorically non-linear). This "non-linearity" is expressed as the specific curvature of an orbital physical-space-time trajectory, to such effect that, as Gauss showed for the orbit of Ceres, that curvature is specific to that orbital or kindred type of trajectory. Hence, from a relatively infinitesimal interval of such an orbit, the entire orbit can be adduced, as Gauss did for Ceres.

43. See Laurence Hecht, et al., "The Significance of the 1845 Gauss-Weber Correspondence," *21st Century Science & Technology*, Fall 1996; pp. 21-43; in *21st Century Science & Technology*, Spring 1997: Dr. Rémi Saumont, "The Battle Over the Laws of Electrodynamics" (pp. 53-60), and Dr. Jonathan Tennenbaum, "Demonstrating Gauss and Weber's Magnetometer" (pp. 61-62). See also Jonathan Tennenbaum, "Die elektrodynamische Revolution von Gauss und Weber," *Fusion*, Vol. 18, No. 1, 1997.

design, which I have just emphasized, above, we must consider the fact that the angular force of Ampère et al., grew out of Ampère's assumptions respecting the roots of electrodynamic action within the scale of the atomic domain, as Weber's crucial-experimental measurements later confirmed this. Ampère's work, like the pioneering work of Sadi Carnot on heat, is rooted in the Leibnizian, and explicitly anti-Newtonian methods of Lazare Carnot, Gaspard Monge, Legendre, et al., in opposition to the blundering Newtonian methods of Cauchy, Clausius, Grassmann, et al. on these same issues of defining the "work" characteristic of both machines and other expressions of crucial-experimental demonstrations of principle.

Now, use the Leibnizian definitions of energy and work employed by Carnot for his treatment of the principles of machine-tool design. This brings to the matter of anti-entropy.

7. The Definition of 'Anti-Entropy'

The term "anti-entropy," was introduced by me, to counter the confusion caused by the unfortunate popularization of Norbert Wiener's fraudulent definition of the term "negentropy," and Wiener's association of that latter term with the nonsensical cabala of "information theory."

Using the terms "energy" and "work" in the same general sense associated with Lazare Carnot's approach to the definitions of design of machines, the rule-of-thumb definition of "anti-entropy," is the following. For general use, the term *anti-entropy* describes the characteristic function of a process, for which the increase of the relevant "energy of the system"/"work" per-capita and per-square-kilometer of the Earth's surface-area, results in a greater rate of increase of the relative "free energy" of that system, to such effect that the ratio of "free energy" to "energy of the system," does not fall, but usually tends to rise.

In physical-economic processes, a characteristically anti-entropic trajectory, is generated in only one way: through the application of improved technologies, which are themselves generated as by-products of validation of newly discovered principles of the universe. The simplest portrait of such a connection is obtained, by tracing the discovery of a new physical principle from its origin in Classical-humanist modes of education, through crucial-experimental validation of a discovered principle, through the application, as improved designs of physical products and physical productive processes, of technologies derived from refined versions of crucial-experimental designs.

The measure of success, or failure, of attempted such trajectories of economic development, is the anti-entropy of the productive process of that society taken as an indivisible whole.

The inputs of such a process (the relevant energy of the system) are measured in either physical units (never money, never money-prices), or, alternately, as rations of both the total labor-force and the total activity of households. All inputs are measured in three respects: 1) Their cost is measured in terms of the current cost of their replacement, that under the *new* conditions of production produced by their consumption; 2) They are also measured, in totality, per capita and per square kilometer, as the levels of total material consumption corresponding to a specific potential relative population-density which that consumption supports for that society taken as an indivisible whole; 3) They are measured, comparatively, in terms of the ration of the total employment of productive labor required to supply the consumption-inputs demanded by the first two considerations.

All of these, and related measurements of cost of a required market-basket of society's total consumption, per capita and per square kilometer, are treated as implicit expressions of a function of anti-entropy. This consumption includes not only household consumption, and costs of production and physical distribution of produced goods, but also improvement and maintenance of all those forms of both "hard" and "social" basic economic infrastructure needed to support a specified level of potential relative population-density and associated anti-entropy. Levels of education required to maintain a rate of potential anti-entropy of the society, are included. So, is the level of investment in basic scientific research required to vector that potential rate of anti-entropy.

In defining such an anti-entropic function for a society as an indivisible whole, the machine-tool factor, and/or equivalent activity, is crucial. In first approximation, the machine-tool factor is approximated by being expressed in terms of the rate of scientific revolutions, as typified by the supercession of an n-fold manifold of physical principles, by an n+1-fold manifold. Actually, it is what I have defined as the "n+m"-fold manifold, which is determining. It is the "n+m"-fold manifold which subsumes the potential machine-tool function within the economic process as a whole.

In practice, as President Franklin Roosevelt's military-agro-industrial mobilization for World War II illustrates the point, what is crucial, is the relative number of qualified scientists effectively mobilized around programs centered upon fundamental research, the number of persons employed as machine-tool and related operatives in machine-tool categories of research and development, and so on.

The essence of all valid forms of modern mathematical physical science, is the development of the ability to define the (relatively) infinitesimal interval of action which defines the trajectory of a process taken in the large. The Classical-Greek root of this notion of mathematical physical science, is the notion of the impossibility of simply mapping a spherical surface to a plane. All valid modern science is traced, on this specific account, from Cardinal Nicholas of Cusa's correction of Archimedes' theorems on quadrature, that the ratio of the circumference of a circular to its diameter, could not be expressed as what Archimedes regarded as an irrational magnitude. This discovery by Cusa, a central feature within his **De docta ignorantia**, is to be appreciated as expressing the axiomatic impossibility of simply mapping a spherical surface to a plane.

That further development within Kepler's development of the first comprehensive mathematical physics, Kepler's expanding appreciation of the implications of the fact that Mars orbit was one of non-constant curvature, established the foundations for all of the principal axiomatic accomplishments of modern mathematical physical science since Kepler. Thus, the characteristic differences expressed in infinitesimal intervals of action, between a spherical and a plane surface, are apprehended as the starting-point for the elaboration of the kind of mathematics required by modern physical science. After Kepler's appreciation of the orbit of Mars, it had to be understood as indispensable, to allow for all possible kinds of non-constant curvatures as the essential states encountered within physical space-time. As Leibniz apprehended the implications of Kepler's proposal for the development of a calculus of the type which Leibniz, alone, originated, no mathematical physical science could be accepted as competent, if it did not derive its mathematical apparatus in conformity with the difference in characteristic curvatures among different physical-space-time trajectories, as reflected in relevant, axiomatically non-linear, characteristic action expressed in infinitesimal intervals of that action.

A factory in McKeesport, Pennsylvania is dynamited—a victim of the shift toward a "post-industrial society." "The entire period, 1966-1998," LaRouche writes, "has been one of ongoing, entropic demolition of the once-powerful and prosperous U.S. economy, a demolition which the counterfeiters of the relevant reporting agencies persisted in reporting as 'continuing strong growth in the economy.'"

This poses the question: This taken into account, what is the characteristic action which defines the anti-entropic physical-space-time trajectory of viable economic processes?

Thus, with that statement, all the sundry pieces of which this report has been composed, now come together as a single, indivisible conception. Now, the significance of the issues posed, for all of science, by the irrationalisms of Kant and Arendt, falls clearly into place. *The characteristic—characteristically anti-entropic quality of—non-linear action, of any viable economic process, is the anti-entropic action located in with the interval defined by a single individual's generation, of a single, validated new principle of our universe.* It is the efficient relationship between that individual's sovereign cognitive action, and the increased power of the entire society in the universe, which is the essential definition of the science of physical economy. The kernel of that characteristic, determining relationship, is expressed in that Riemannian form of multiply-connected manifold, "n+m," we have identified above.

It is, therefore, the sovereign cognitive action of the individual mind, which expresses, as an infinitesimal, the elementary form of characteristic action determining the "curvature" of that physical-economic space-time. The typical such action is reflected in the multiply-connected interaction of such sovereign forms of individual cognitive processes.

It is not necessary to generate a calculated value for this typical such action; it is indispensable that one's comprehension of the physical-economic process be premised upon a comprehension of the nature of this multiply-connected interaction. It is indispensable that we appreciate the manner in which changes in this typical value are to be brought about, and employ measurements of a reasonably estimated relative rate of anti-entropy so effected.

This epistemological setting of the determination of functional trajectories of economic policy-shaping, is the kernel of my original discoveries in economic science. It was this breakthrough, respecting the determining role of epistemological considerations, which was necessary, at last, to reach the level at which economics becomes science.

From this vantage-point, one should be able to recognize two relevant points, that more or less immediately.

a. That there is a reciprocal relationship between the contemplative and linear standpoint of oligarchism, on the one side, and the types of axiomatic assumptions associated with Descartes and his empiricist followers in the anti-Kepler, anti-Leibniz faction of science.

b. Since what Leibniz defined as non-constant curvature in the infinitesimally small, is the characteristic feature of both physical processes in general, and physical-economic processes in particular, no one could tolerate the empiricist and related contemplative views of physical-science matters, and also tolerate a competent approach to ascertaining the principled underlying features of physical-economic processes.

Thus, the toleration of neo-Aristotelean and empiricist mind-sets, is the efficient root of those habits of opinion-shaping which foster modern society's worst economic catastrophes, such as the present one. "Thus, conscience [disguised as customary opinion] makes cowards of them all."

As I cautioned those engaged in constructing estimates of U.S. economic performance, under the 1979-1983 operations preparing the *EIR Quarterly Economic Forecast,* the ups and downs of the relative anti-entropy of the economic process appear as determined by a kind of step-function. The changes in the national economy which correspond to such step-functions, reflect either an upgrading or downgrading of the relevant, estimable Riemannian manifold. That is to say, that either effective principles are being added to, or deducted from the effective functioning of that economy.

During 1979-1983, for example, the collapse of the U.S. economy, at real-economy rates, effectively, of two percent per year or more, reflected chiefly the impact of the structural changes in the U.S. economy implemented under the Trilateral Commission program carried out by the Carter Administration, as continued means of such degenerative measures as continued "deregulation," Volcker measures, Garn-St Germain, Kemp-Roth, etc., during the first Reagan Administration. These structural changes complemented those begun during 1966-1967 under President Johnson, the continuing, disastrously devolutionary impact of 1971-1972 institution of a global "floating exchange-rate" monetary order, and the oil-price-hoax swindle of the mid-1970s.

The changes in the U.S. economy which occurred during the 1975-1983 interval, had the effect of one Riemannian "slab," after the other, peeling off from the U.S. real economy, and dropping into oblivion. The entire period, 1966-1998, has been one of ongoing, entropic demolition of the once-powerful and prosperous U.S. economy, a demolition which the counterfeiters of the relevant reporting agencies persisted in reporting as "continuing strong growth in the economy." It is the cancer, not the healthy tissue, which has been doing the growing. "Free trade" and "globalization" have put the entire U.S. economy on the economic garbage-dump.

Thus, the typical anti-entropy (or, entropy) of the economic process, rooted in the "infinitesimal" Riemannian changes of the state of the sovereign cognitive processes of the individual, determines the relative physical-economic space-time curvature of the real economic process as a whole, just as Gauss's measurements determined the asteroid orbits in the large. It is attention to what has been identified here as the relevant Riemannian function, which provides us the point of reference from which to define efficient and effective shaping of national and international economic policies.

8. What Stopped Newton's Clock?

Competent economic policy-shaping proceeds from emphasis upon two phases of the multiply-connected relations among the sovereign cognitive processes of the individual persons: 1. The fostering of the development, or the repression of those cognitive processes as such; 2. the fostering of the realization of scientific and related individual progress in the medium of economic and related social relations.

Neo-Aristoteleanism and empiricism typify the still-broader use of irrationalism as a policy for aborting the social and related effects of scientific and technological progress. Under a sane economic policy, the possibility of scientific and technological progress is a self-evident imperative for the shaping of economic and related policies. Under the forms of neo-Aristoteleanism and empiricism which are implemented in aid of keeping large rations of humanity in the condition of virtual human cattle, the very existence of willful scientific and related progress is either denied outrightly (as in empiricism), or is degraded to nothing less disgusting than a merely possible topic of cognitive, logical contemplation. Under the sway of existentialism, or the related satanic policies of Britain's Duke of Edinburgh and his World Wildlife Fund and "world religion" project, progress has been, since 1961, implicitly prohibited.

These same epistemological issues of policy-shaping are expressed in the guise of educational policies. The anti-Classical-humanist reforms of education, which were dictated by the Paris office of the OECD organization, under Dr. Alexander King, and the implementation of those OECD and "Frankfurt School" policies under the title of the so-called "Brandt reforms" in education in Germany, are typical. Also expressing the same pathologies in educational policies, are the Yahoo policies of education currently popular in the U.S.A., that education should become virtually optional, or limited to providing the student training for whatever menial form of employment has been chosen for that student, in advance.

Thus, we have the common connection of the otherwise dissimilar cases of Kant and Arendt. We have, to the same effect, the Yahoo policies of the leading mass-media of most of today's world, such as the *Washington Post*, the British Commonwealth's Hollinger and Murdoch chains, and the ongoing, abortive schemes for elevating the Internet to the role of George Orwell's fictional "Big Brother."

Similarly, we see the sundry proposals for economic policies which will degrade the children and grandchildren of today's young-adult populations into snarls of monkey-like, mass-rutting Yahoos. The anti-progress freaks' cry is out, and loud: "Stop government-sponsored basic scientific research! Stop public funding of space exploration! Eliminate large-scale public infrastructure programs! Establish international supervision to hold back all forms of technological progress presumptively. Legalize stupefaction of populations through allegedly 'harm-reducing' modes of free distribution of mind-dulling substances!" (After all, what person could protest against the loss of the mind whose former presence it can no longer remember?)

Above all, today's would-be "Big Brother" proposes, "Ban truth and sanity alike, all in the holy name of 'democracy.'" The resulting reduction of the human mind to linearity, in its resulting, infinitesimal littleness, were better named "globulization," than "globalization." What has ruined the once-prosperous U.S.A.'s economy, is not only insane in its effects; its effects are determined by the insanity introduced to the mind of an increasing ration of our populations, as the case of the sodden Immanuel Kant and evil Hannah Arendt merely typify such forms of insanity.

It is by establishing stupidity, or even lunacy, as customary public opinion, that nations, even entire cultures, are induced to destroy themselves. Under such forms of democracy, the people become their own tyrant, and destroy themselves. So, Newton's clock stopped, as his mentor, "Samiel" Clarke, suggested it would.

What Happened at Novosibirsk?

From the outbreak of that present, terminal phase of the planetary financial crisis, which erupted in October 1997, as I had forewarned it would, until late November 1998, the effective response from the so-called G-7 nations, has been collectively insane. Despite some interesting, scattered statements uttered by U.S. President Bill Clinton, the G-7 nations have done nothing that was not, in effect, worse than had they done nothing at all. By mid-1998, it became apparent to an increasing number of the leading forces in Asia, that "The Mantle of Heaven" had fallen away from not only pathetic Director Michel Camdessus's IMF, but also the governments of western Europe, the U.S.A., and Canada. Some of the influential passengers lost confidence in the leadership provided by the captain of the world's sinking economic *Titanic*; with each passing day, more nations are indicating their thoughts about jumping ship, as the hyperinflationary charade of the past weeks disgusts even some among those central bankers who launched this foolish prank.

So, it became evident, during recent weeks, that the role of leadership must pass from the G-7's to saner hands, probably to a group of Eurasia nations gathered in cooperation with initiatives radiating from the present government of China.[44] Thus, the most portentous political earthquake of the past half-century, the earth-shaking address delivered by China's President Jiang Zemin at Russia's famous science-city, Novosibirsk, came and passed, almost without notice in the mass-media of the self-doomed western Europe and U.S.A. The very fact that the President of China went there to deliver a keynote address was already of historic importance; the content of that address shook the heavens. A sullen mass-media of western Europe and the U.S.A.—otherwise better known as the customarily lying press—mumbled a few grumpy, geopolitical threats, but otherwise adhered strictly to the dictum:

Speak not of the rope in the house of the hanged!

For several centuries, since the middle of the Eighteenth Century, western Europe's modern civilization has dominated the world, increasingly, until a more than a quarter-century process of degeneration of those nations' economies, beginning the first half of the 1970s. Although the Anglo-American, trans-Atlantic arrangement has continued to dominate the world, the collapse of the net per-capita productive powers of labor of this region, since approximately the time of the inauguration of the Trilateral Commission's U.S. President Jimmy Carter, has imparted to so-called "Western civilization" what the Welsh call the fey look of a doomed empire in decline, like the fallen empires of Mesopotamia, Rome, Byzantium, and the Habsburgs, of the past.

Until recently, especially after the abrupt, 1989-1991 collapse of the Soviet Union's power, it appeared to credulous observers, that Prime Minister Margaret Thatcher and her toady George Bush, had emerged from the ruins of blasted Panama and Iraq, as powers so greatly strengthened by those events, that they would continue to be the unchallengeable masters of the planet, for a long time yet to come. Nonetheless, with the developments in world financial markets since October 1997, that illusory image of unchallengeable Anglo-American power has, like the image of the fabled Cheshire Cat, faded considerably; the cat's smile is, indeed, at the point it might vanish suddenly, leaving an empty branch of the tree as sole reminder of the fact that it had once been there. The blundering and bungling of the governments of the G-7 nations, since mid-September of this year, have brought matters to the present point, that even the childish dreams of a spontaneous recovery in U.S. and western European financial markets, will soon end forever, as the full force of the now-onrushing phase of this crisis hits with increasing, terrible force, during the eight-week period of collapse immediately ahead.

The psychological turning-point came between President Clinton's Sept. 14, 1998 bold address to the New York Council on Foreign Relations, and the weak-kneed response on the same issues following the victory of the so-called "red-green coalition" in the Sept. 27 general election in Germany. In between those dates, the Sept. 23 collapse of the Long-Term Capital Management (LTCM) bubble, and the onrushing fears of an impending Brazil crisis, appeared to have broken Clinton's will to launch serious initiatives addressing the causes

---

44. Recent statements by LaRouche on China, Russia, and India include the following from *Executive Intelligence Review*: "Toward a New Bretton Woods" (March 27, 1998; text of a speech to an *EIR* seminar in Washington, D.C. on March 18); "Russia: A Coup from Above" (April 3, 1998); "There Is No Possible Bail-Out of the World Financial System" (April 24, from a radio interview with "EIR Talks," April 14, 1998); "Mathematics & Measurement: Science vs. Ideology" (Aug. 21, 1998); "LaRouche: We Must Provide Leadership" (Sept. 18; text of a speech delivered by audiotape to a conference of the Schiller Institute in Reston, Virginia, on Sept. 5); "Time to Tell the Truth" (Oct. 16, 1998); and "Is Western Europe Doomed?" (Nov. 27, 1998).

of the global crisis.[45] Under what were fairly described as highly visible, and also hysterical pressures from Blair fanatic and U.S. Vice-President Al Gore, the President fell into what will probably turn out to be a temporary alliance with his enemy, Britain's now increasingly shaky, "Third Way" Prime Minister, Tony Blair.[46]

Whatever President Clinton may do next, his evasion of the actual nature of the present global crisis, has done grave damage to his influence since the disastrous early October Washington, D.C. sessions of the G-7. There, the so-called "European," supranational-government approach of Britain's Tony Blair was, in effect, inserted into the mouth of President Clinton. In such matters, the President is the victim of self-inflicted wounds; sometimes, it is the failure to act, which may prove to be the politically fatal, self-inflicted wound. Whatever fears might have constrained the President from effective action, he should have feared the consequences of giving in to his fears more than any other threat to his Presidency, the U.S.A., or civilization.

Whatever the President's reasons—the legendary Miniver Cheevy's, Gore's, or his own—his failure to respond in an appropriate and timely way, posed the question to the world at large: "If the U.S. President refuses to act with a responsible initiative, to shut down the system that is killing the world, who will?"

My associates and I have been faced with this question many times, during the U.S. Presidency's flipping and flopping on unpostponable, life-death issues, during the recent years and months—especially since Spring 1996. My wife and I, among other collaborators, had made our views on this question clear, repeatedly, as I did once more in my *EIR* report: "Is Western Europe Doomed?", and as I did in a Nov. 21, 1998 address to a Bad Schwalbach conference. My answer has been: the only possible alternative is a leadership initiative among a group of Asian nations, all centered around cooperation with China, and, hopefully, including Russia.

During recent weeks, not only China and Malaysia, but other important nations, outside of western Europe and the U.S.A., have taken a hopeful and serious attitude towards the new situation in Eurasia. The role of China's government has been crucial in inspiring such more independent and optimistic changes in spirit and attitude. In this setting, President Jiang Zemin's Nov. 24, 1998 address at Novosibirsk,[47] has the utmost strategic significance for those hopeful of an early alternative to the global breakdown crisis which President Clinton has been unwilling, so far, to face.

The recent and impending meetings among a group of nations, including China with Russia, China with Japan, and Russia with India, reflect the emergence of a crucial new potential for the planet as a whole. These developments are to be studied in light of two primary background considerations, to both of which your attention will be devoted in this closing section of the report. Also noted, and also strategically relevant, but on the negative side, is the lack, so far, of any competent public reporting on these developments, from among the governments and leading mass media of western Europe and the United States.

Russia, China, and India typify the relatively most powerful among a group of nations long considered to be "outsiders" to the trans-Atlantic axis of world power, outside the Anglo-American-dominated, G-7 "Club." As either "Communist" states, or "developing nations," or both, these outsiders have been treated as "inferior" in morals and culture to the leading powers of so-called "Western civilization." With the collapse of the Soviet Union, the myth was, that this development had "proven" beyond question the intrinsic superiority of the "free trade" to the "dirigistic" systems; besides, it was believed, that no one potential objector was powerful enough to contest the virtually dictatorial authority assumed by what it was believed that the Thatcher-Bush concert of Anglo-American world-ruling powers had established during developments of 1990-1991.

On this account, especially after 1989-1991, both the former associates of the Soviet Union and the so-called "developing nations" were, in fact, so much defeated by their own fears of Anglo-American invincibility, that they preferred to be unaware of the actual, in

<hr>

45. Lyndon H. LaRouche, Jr., "Food, Not Money, Is the Crisis," *Executive Intelligence Review*, Nov. 13, 1998. Notably, the current, "red-green" German government, has been shaky since even before the government was actually installed, and appears to be growing shakier with each passing round of developments since. See Lyndon H. LaRouche, Jr., "Is Western Europe Doomed?" *Executive Intelligence Review*, Nov. 27, 1998.

46. Notably, the role of Gore and Blair in attempting to push the U.S. into Blair's screeching demands for an indefinite period of mass bombing of Iraq, followed by Gore's disgusting performance at the Kuala Lumpur APEC meeting, has cooled White House relations with Blair considerably, and may have doomed Vice-President Gore's Year 2000 Presidential aspirations. Nonetheless, what happened between Sept. 23 and President Clinton's pull-back from the Iraq bombing, has done tremendous damage to the President's earlier position of authority among nations of Asia and elsewhere. See Mary Burdman, "Gore Bombs at APEC," *Executive Intelligence Review*, Nov. 27, 1998.

47. See report and English translation of the text of address, under Mary Burdman, "Jiang in Russia: A Speech That Can Change History," *Executive Intelligence Review*, Dec. 4, 1998.

fact, waning of that supposed invincibility. As former India Prime Minister Jawaharlal Nehru points to this factor, in his autobiography, the British Raj did this with its India colony, the occupying powers relying less upon the forces at their disposal, than upon instilling a sense of inferiority in those whom they dominated and looted.[48] Then, with the October 1997 outbreak of the present, terminal phase of the global financial crisis, a deep and fundamental change was introduced to the situation. The disgraceful failure of the U.S.A. and western European governments, in face of the challenge presented by developments of the August-October 1998 interval, showed to the world that the supposed giant of the Atlantic Alliance still had a nasty fist, but was otherwise "a giant with a head of clay." The growing sense of the political ineptitude of the governments of the trans-Atlantic powers, prompted what was partly a psychological change, but a change with profound, epoch-making dimensions.

The essence of this recent change is captured by the content and implications of President Jiang Zemin's Nov. 24 address at Novosibirsk. Neither President Clinton, nor any other present head of state or government, or leading political party in western Europe or the U.S.A., would have been capable, either emotionally or intellectually, of even conceptualizing the implications of that Novosibirsk address. Indeed, the press and related reaction from official leaders of the trans-Atlantic powers, presented a spectacle of ill-tempered, and very small-minded Lilliputians snarling and spitting at a giant Lemuel Gulliver. The contrast is between a China awakened, and moving forward as a young giant might, and, on the other side, a decadent, doomed, and morose collection of relics of dying trans-Atlantic power succumbing to probably fatal, self-inflicted cultural wounds. The threat to these decadent trans-Atlantic powers, does not come from Asia; it comes only from the fatal corruption which has, for the past thirty years, hitherto dominated, increasingly, the political parties and financial establishments of those decaying powers themselves.

Situate the apparent strategic issues so posed, and then reexamine the implications of Jiang Zemin's address in that light.

---

48. In connection with India, North Americans and Europeans usually underrate the crucial role of Bal Gangadhar Tilak, in breaking the Congress Party free from the British control which Annie Besant typified. Tilak did this by scholarly attacks on the British myth of India's cultural inferiority at the myth's most vulnerable point, by exploding the (in fact) baseless bit of imperial fiction, that modern civilization had originated with the work of Mesopotamian Semitic tribes.

Listen to the speeches from the putatively leading spokesmen for the decaying trans-Atlantic powers, for the decadent G-7, for example. Listen to the hysterical overtones of their petulant hissing and spitting. They say, in chorus, words to the effect: "You may think that you could change our minds. We are committed to the post-industrial world-order we are now consolidating. You will never reverse our established 'free trade' and 'globalization' policies. We have established these trends, and they are now irreversible." So, the Persian Emperor might have sent his dire warning to Alexander the Great: "We will meet you on the plains outside Arbela!" Such speeches, and they are routine from those quarters these days, call up images of famous King Canute railing against the wind and waves, images of Belshazzar's Feast. These governments and leading political parties of the trans-Atlantic powers have surely gone utterly, suicidally mad!

China's efforts are not directed to conquering "the West." That is not the conflict. China's efforts are directed, plainly and simply, to surviving, despite the trans-Atlantic powers' presently manifest commitment to mass economic and cultural suicide. The threats which the Hollinger and other British media direct against China, Malaysia, Russia, and other nations today, is: "Join our suicide-pact, or else we will kill you."

The policies which President Jiang Zemin has recently affirmed, to Russia and Japan, most notably, are policies designed to enable China and as many other nations as choose to do so, to join in cooperation for global survival of the onrushing imminent collapse of not only the financial systems, but also the physical economies of most, if not all of the nations and regions of this planet. China's corresponding, stated, and practiced foreign policy is fashioned on principally three most obvious components, all matched by a cohering domestic policy for China's internal development.

Looking from East to West, from the eastern port-terminal in China's Lianyungang, to Rotterdam, the policy is to develop a trans-Eurasian Land-Bridge, a conduit of railways and correlated other infrastructural links, opening up the internal regions of Eurasia for an economic development which will be revolutionary in its economic impact for Eurasia as a whole. This is a revival of the proposal originally developed by the German-American economist Friedrich List.

This Eurasia Land-Bridge spine is complemented by the build-up of a proposed partnership among the nations immediately affected by the Land-Bridge program, from Japan to Rotterdam, and embracing the nations of most of Asia and continental Europe, all in a scheme of cooperation centered upon the leading economies of Asia, Japan, China, India, and Russia, with special consideration for the nations of Southeast Asia.

The third key feature of the foreign economic and related policies brings the Novosibirsk address into sharper focus.

These leading facets of China's economic foreign policy, are matched by the commitment to elevate the entire population of China itself to a world standard by early during the coming century. Those combined and interdependent elements of China's foreign and domestic economic policy bring our attention now to the crucial concluding point of this report.

For reasons of economic science which have been stressed in this report, the successful realization of China's policies for economic cooperation with its prospective Land-Bridge partners, depends upon a massive mobilization of science-driver programs of machine-tool and related technological development. Given the scope of such needs among China and other nations of Asia as a whole, the success of the entire economic policy depends upon a science-driver and machine-tool mobilization on a scale and with an intensity never before undertaken on this planet. For this purpose, the former Soviet Union's scientific-military-industrial complex, as exemplified by Novosibirsk, is an indispensable component. This policy is the only hope for Russia; it defines an environment which is indispensable for India. It is presently, the only source of economic hope for the nearly smashed economy of western Europe. The entire world needs this policy, urgently; only such cooperation, of this intensity, on this scale, can reverse the plunge toward doom which has been unleashed upon us now, by the foolish choices of policy-directions adopted by the trans-Atlantic powers during the recent thirty-odd years.

President Jiang Zemin's Novosibirsk address, thus addresses every practical implication of the discussion of economic science featured in this report.

Economics must now, finally, become truly economic science. That economic science must be the policy of cooperation among the sovereign nation-states of this planet throughout the coming century.